MW01173450

HIGH CALLING

A Training Manual for Men of God and Ladies of Grace

Lon and Kay Chenowith

High Calling
Copyright © 2016 by Lon and Kay Chenowith. All rights reserved.
Copyright © 2021 by Lon and Kay Chenowith. All rights reserved.

No part of this publication may be reproduced, stored in a retrieval system or transmitted in any way by any means, electronic, mechanical, photocopy, recording or otherwise without the prior permission of the author except as provided by USA copyright law. Scripture quotations are taken from the Holy Bible, King James Version, Cambridge, 1769. Used by permission. All rights reserved.

Book design by Mary Reynolds
Book Cover Photograph: Spitzkoppe Natural Reserve, Namibia, by Michael, Adobe Photostock
Interior images: jeffjacobs, Pixabay.com; waldryano, Pixabay.com; jean52, Pixabay.com; Adobe Photostock licensed images; http://clipart.christiansunite.com/

Published in the United States of America

ISBN: 978-1-68301-926-8
ISBN: 979-8-73412-661-5 Second Edition
1. Religion / Christian Life / Stewardship /Leadership
2. Religion / Christian Ministry / General

16.07.22

This book is dedicated to the men of God in Sandy Run Baptist Association, Bostic, North Carolina

TABLE OF CONTENTS

ACKNOWLEDGEMENTS

We acknowledge the God-called men and women who are faithful to the Gospel ministry. They are warriors who know spiritual warfare and affirm that the battle is the Lord's (2 Chronicles 20:15). They are intercessors who render heartfelt prayers. They are servants who endure heartaches to advance the kingdom of heaven. Their cause is the glory of God and the salvation of souls.

We thank the men of God in Sandy Run Baptist Association.

Heartfelt thanks to the families of the men of God who share in their calling. They are wives who take delight when souls are saved and hearts are transformed—yet persevere through the long days of a minister's life. They are sons and daughters who see the upside when God works and the downside of dealing with broken hearts and imperfect lives.

We're thankful for those ladies who encourage their pastor husbands.

Above all, we acknowledge the Master, who is beyond compare. Without him, ministers can do nothing (John 15:5). He is life. In him they move and have their being (Acts 17:28). He gives the Holy Spirit and the mighty Word of God. He provides supernatural gifts to serve his people.

We especially acknowledge the Master for the gift of his shepherding grace.

Thanks to the men of God who edited this book from its rough beginnings: Dr. Bill Oakley, Dr. Steve Gouge, Pastor Kipp Roten, Pastor Matty Ponce de Leon, and Dr. Mack Tester. These are what the Bible calls "true men" in character, love, and encouragement.

PREFACE

For I have not shunned to declare
unto you all the counsel of God.
—Acts 20:27

When Paul left the Ephesian church, he left them with a call to courage and prophetic warnings. Acts 20:27 reveals that what he shared was not by his own invention but by the inspiration of the Holy Spirit. The whole counsel of God is found in the Bible. That is the authority of this working manual for men of God and ladies of grace, who serve the Lord on the front lines.

Many will take exception to what they read here. The appeal is to the Word of God—not to the culture, not to politically correct social positions. But what does the Word of God teach in its purest form? If offense is taken, be certain that the conflict is not with biblical truth. The godly are always willing to be corrected if what they have been taught is not affirmed by the Word of God.

The Bereans as described in Acts 17:10-11 were "more noble" because they searched the scriptures to see if what they were being taught was true.

And the brethren immediately sent away Paul and Silas by night unto Berea: who coming thither went into the synagogue of the Jews. These were more noble than those in Thessalonica, in that they received the word with all readiness of mind, and searched the scriptures daily, whether those things were so.

Let us be Bereans! Many will bristle at the teaching on the qualifications for men of God, women in ministry, and spiritual gifts. Be careful about raw opinion rather than relying upon revealed truth.

When it comes to the difficult issue of the truth of miracles, healings, and tongues, the Word of God is clear about what is out of bounds. Many charismatic practices are out of bounds. There are many true brothers and sisters in their ranks, but the error of idolizing personalities is not the same as honoring God. It is a grief to His Spirit.

Based on the timeline in the New Testament and on the practice of spiritual gifts through the millenniums of historic Christian faith, there is a distinction in the church between the first century and what follows. All legitimate evangelicals limit direct revelation of the scripture to the apostles. Most do not accept apostolic authority thereafter.

What is happening today in the church is not only dangerous but also blasphemous and devilish. To believe that there are men who speak for God apart from the scriptures, that men and women could believe that their words are like those of God so that they can speak things into being... That is clear heresy. Too many forget that Jesus warned of such in the last days.

The goal is to be as close to the scriptures as possible, not only in belief but also in practice. There is much in the church today that is unquestioned even though it is "off the map" when compared to biblical authority and the New Testament model.

What is the New Testament model? That is what we intend to explore so that we can understand the divine standard. We know the blessing of God is on those who obey him (Matthew 7:21, Revelation 22:14).

A church is as sound as it is in keeping with scripture. Churches exist in incredible numbers that deny the virgin birth and the bodily resurrection. Those churches are better seen as clubs because they are a far cry from the church of the New Testament. Denying any tenet of historic Christian faith is a denial of the Lord Jesus and his redemptive work.

A host of churches dot the landscape that embrace what is called the Prosperity Doctrine—the belief that God wants his people to be healthy and wealthy. Somehow the Master and the apostles missed that message! It is heresy because it is materialistic and man-centered. Men and women fleece the gullible with this flamboyant teaching as a show to feed their egos and greed.

Movements can be guilty of teaching that they are the only ones that get it right and are going to heaven. Many allow church traditions to overshadow the truth of the Bible. The most disturbing dynamic is the disparity of those who say that they love the Lord yet live like the devil—no, this isn't limited to those who drink and abuse drugs, but this extends to the malicious gossips and the self-righteous.

Such blatant hypocrisy has been an age-old trouble in the church, but it is still shocking to see how blinded people are to attitudes and behaviors that are so contrary to the true Christian faith. That is not to say that proper righteous standards are out of place. The challenge is in those who seem to be oblivious to the wickedness of self-righteousness and a harsh, critical spirit.

Culture will be referenced often. It is applied in two ways: church culture and the country's culture. Culture is not evil, but at any given time it can have a downward drift or an upward bent. The Christian leader's call is to point both the church and country's cultures heavenward.

A pure Gospel ministry is not for stone throwers. It is for humble, soul-loving people who believe righteousness comes from Christ and that his standards are the standards that his people hold dear. His love is impartial, but once his grace and mercy comes to a soul, that life is forever changed. Pure Gospel ministry revels in truth and rejoices in love. This kind of ministry submits totally to the authority of the scripture, so much so that the evolving culture is put in check. The question should not be "What is popular?" but rather "What is acceptable, pleasing, and right in the Lord's eyes?" It is the standard stated in Romans 12:2:

> And be not conformed to this world: but be ye transformed by the re-newing of your mind, that ye may prove what is that good, and acceptable, and perfect, will of God.

The aim of these pages is just that: to appeal to him and to discover the truth of the Bible.

INTRODUCTION

And when the chief Shepherd shall appear, ye shall receive a crown of glory that fadeth not away.—1 Peter 5:4

The crown of glory is one of five crowns named in the New Testament. The four others are the incorruptible crown, the crown of rejoicing, the crown of righteousness, and the crown of life. The crown of glory is for pastors (elders, bishops, and men of God) who serve the people of God in the Word, doctrine, and prayer.

These men of God do not serve for filthy lucre, lord over God's heritage, fail to be an example, tickle the ear, neglect evangelism, or dismiss the commands of the Lord. They oversee the church and prepare the people of God for the judgment seat of Christ.

True shepherds are scarce. Few men of God stand against the wolves and rescue the lambs. Fewer still will sacrifice themselves for the sheep to keep unity and truth prevalent in the fellowship. Even a smaller percentage will exalt Jesus and extol his name above theirs and their reputation. Yet the Lord is calling such men and placing them in churches where the candle of truth still burns. Though there may be few men who meet the biblical model and many churches are already apostate (have fallen away from loving and obeying Jesus), God is faithful to send true shepherds.

The apostle Peter wrote as a fellow elder to the early church. He was an eyewitness of Christ's sufferings and a partaker of his glory. First Peter 5:1-4 gives direct instructions to every man of God so that there is a clear picture of obedience for those who honor the text.

- Feed the flock of God.
- Take the oversight.
- Be examples to the flock.

<table>
<tr><td>

These are the scriptural mandates. For those who serve the church as undershepherds, Peter says that when the chief Shepherd shall appear, they shall receive a crown of glory (1 Peter 5:4). There is no question who the chief Shepherd is. He's the one who laid down his life for the sheep (John 10:11, 15, 17–18).

The man of God is marked by how he shepherds. He is to protect, guide, and lead the sheep all the way up to the tableland—that is, the rich pastures upon the mountaintops. The people of God should not be led by other people's messages, but with the very Word of God forged in the preacher's heart.

It is no secret that the church is in a mess. God has called men to lead his church as a ministry, not a business. He does not seek populists but those who say without equivocation "Thus saith the Lord." God wants men of vision—not just dreamers but those who have a vision of his glory.

Men of God feed the flock with truth in love (Ephesians 4:15). They are born-again believers gifted to lead. Pastors who follow the New Testament understand that deacons are qualified to serve, not to lead. They know churches that operate by democratic rule do so because of culture, not apostolic faith.

Shepherds have no leadership if they have no example. Peter says shepherds cannot serve for "filthy lucre." They cannot be little lords. They recalled by heaven to model the Christian life in the family and in the Christian community. (Paul lists the qualifications with clear parameters in 1 Timothy 3:1–7 and Titus 1:5–9.)

The church is hard-pressed to find such men today. It is common for pastors' children to be hellions. Such men are unquestionably disqualified. It seems we have forgotten 1 Timothy 3:5:

> *For if a man know not how to rule his own house, how shall he take care of the church of God?*

Whenever leadership is compromised in the church, it affects the Gospel witness in the community. Men who are immoral, dishonest, and egotistical are not qualified to lead people to heaven. The people of God are hurting

</td><td>

Notes

</td></tr>
</table>

for true shepherds who love truth, serve in grace, and walk with the Lord.

There can be no crowns of glory if God's glory is not seen in the church through godly leaders who feed, lead, and model the Christian life. Many men are faithful and true yet at the same time, are maligned. God has promised them a crown. They are akin to their Master and to the apostles!

So how does the church find such men? Many around the world look to where there is a record of success, growth, and an impressive pedigree. But those are not what God deems important. Men of God contend for the faith and love to share amazing grace. They are holy men who are tried and tempered.

These men are practical. They know how to lead a heart to forgiveness and make things right. Their Bibles are worn because they have marked them up and wept over them. They know the power of prayer. They understand when it is time to be peaceful and where to draw the line.

These men love their wives and raise godly children. They are not perfect but are humble men still reaching for holiness. They love people because they love souls. True pastors do not have a big appetite for just food, amusement, or thrills. They hunger to do the will of the Father and to please him in all things.

They are called shepherds because they take care of the sheep. They feed, protect, and nurture them. Sheep nuzzle them and follow them. Wolves and bears are afraid of them, and goats butt them! The shepherd leads the sheep to green pastures and still waters.

May the Lord give the church of this age true shepherds who serve under His watchful eye. A good verse to remember is Hebrews 13:20-21:

> *Now the God of peace, that brought again from the dead our Lord Jesus,*
> *that great shepherd of the sheep, through the blood of the everlasting*
> *covenant, Make you perfect in every good work to do his will, working in*
> *you that which is well pleasing in his sight, through Jesus Christ; to whom*
> *be glory for ever and ever. Amen.*

Summary Statements:

1. Men who are immoral, dishonest, and egotistical are not qualified to lead people to heaven.
2. The men qualified to do so are practical. They know how to lead a heart to forgiveness and make things right.

How are such men found?

They are found at work in the church. Such men are faithful in practical ministries. They are men who spend time in prayer, labor, and weep over their Bibles. These kinds of men are priests in their own homes, leading their wives and children in family devotions. The Word of God burns like a fi re in their bones (Jeremiah 20:9).

Can the sins of another person (e.g., a family member) disqualify a God-called man from serving as a pastor?

Yes, if we honor the teaching of 1 Timothy 3:4-5 and Titus1:6. The Bible is clear about the criteria for service in those verses. Each church will take one of two positions: they will take or leave the scripture based on the situation, or they will line up with God's standard.

Do the actions of a man of God's adult children disqualify him?

The pastoral epistles do not have a point-blank answer to this question, but the standard of the biblical text is high. It is easy to make exceptions for a variety of situations. If they have been raised in the Christian faith and now live the lifestyle of an unbeliever, the family would no longer serve as an example of the faith. Most would apply 1 Timothy 3:4-5 and Titus 1:6 to the children still in the home, not adult children that are grown and gone, but the Titus passage still calls for faithful children.

Can disqualified men ever be qualified again?

No. It is difficult to meet the high standard of pastoral leadership once they have been disqualified. If they have been immoral or unethical, their reputation would be known in the church and throughout the community. Such men can go through a process to return to ministry—just not pastoral ministry. This is no less true for deacon ministry.

Notes

Part 1

A Profile of Spiritual Leadership

Chapter 1

Qualifications

The New Testament character traits for a pastor and his family can be taken as a set of standards or suggestions. However, the contemporary church views much of the Bible as more of the latter than the former. Heaven's high calling to Christian ministry requires God—not man—to determine the caliber of leadership. At times men can work at the lowest level. But God never does.

This day is one of low standards and little accountability for ministry. The list of character traits for men of God are found in 1 Timothy 3:1-7 and Titus 1:5-9. For any church fully committed to obeying the scriptures, this is not optional. The world has become a place where people see preachers as impure, dishonest, and egotistical. Any of those charges disqualifies them.

If God's people want the Father's blessing on the work of the church, they will align the church with the teachings of the New Testament. Whenever there is confusion, disorder, and a poor testimony for the church in the community, it's an indication that the Word has been breached somewhere.

There is an alarming number of churches that are revolting against pastoral leadership, and these churches are led by those who believe that they are just as qualified to direct the work of the church as pastors are—even though they do not have the calling or the gifts to do so. The result is a great disservice to the people of God, confusion, and a loss of excellence in doing the work of the church. There are at least four qualifications in church leadership.

The Man of God is Devoted to His Family

The first qualification is that the shepherd must have his family in order. As previously stated, "For if a man know not how to rule his own house, how shall he take care of the church of God?" (1 Timothy 3:5). If his marriage is not right and his wife is not qualified for and called to ministry, he is not qualified to be a pastor. If his children are unruly, rebellious, and irreverent, he's not qualified.

There goes the majority of the men in the ministry! The church is in trouble because pastors who lead them are poor examples and are not qualified as spiritual leaders. It is common for men to make exceptions and excuses for talented speakers and so-called good men who have bad families. God, however, does not. He expects his men to put the faith in practice or to step down!

That requires pastors to make their families their first place of ministry and their children their first line of disciples. If they cannot get the message across at home, they cannot do so in the church. One of the best witnesses church leaders can have is to take immoral, unethical, and arrogant men out of the ministry and replace them with pure, true, and humble men of God.

No man is perfect, but there are standards of righteousness every man must uphold. How can we expect the world to believe the testimony of the church if the people of God cannot clean up their act and be governed by legitimate leadership? Hear the words of Nathan to King David: "Howbeit, because by this deed thou hast given great occasion to the enemies of the Lord to blaspheme..." (2 Samuel 12:14).

The Man of God has Knowledge of the Word

Preachers can be good storytellers and comedians—not always competent Bible teachers who make the Word of God come alive. The Bible is the source of counsel, evangelism, discipleship, and leadership. It is hard to please the Lord if the model for ministry is charismatic personalities, culturally-accommodating churches, and doing church as if it is only a business.

The Old and New Testaments are both necessary. It is difficult for people to get a hold of grace if they do not understand the Law. The preacher's heroes ought to be biblical heroes. Get to know Zephaniah, for example, and the major message of this minor prophet. (Don't miss Zephaniah 3:17, though keep in mind that the preacher's worldview is to be Christian, which comes from the New Testament.)

The man of God's mind and heart ought to be saturated with the Bible. He should know it from cover to cover, theme by theme, and principle on top of principle. The Holy Spirit-inspired text is enduring and inerrant in its original form. God preserved it. The Bible preacher is responsible to submit and surrender his life and ministry to obey it.

Notes

When the Word of God is proclaimed, the preacher must be sure that he is preaching it in context, keeping with the truths of all scripture, and know that it is the very source of moral and spiritual authority. Human opinion is irrelevant. There is one true interpretation of scripture; and the preacher should do all he can to proclaim it, regardless of the cost.

The Man of God is Courageous

This may be the lost leadership quality in the church today. Too many Christian fellowships are ruled by the ungodly through political manipulation. It is always wrong for men who are not committed to prayer and have not paid the price of practical ministry and lived out the truths of the Bible to be given license to oversee a church. Pastors are to be examples of courageous service.

Many will wonder why only men have been noted for pastoral leadership. That's because they're the only ones indicated in scripture. It is a breach of the sacred text to add or take away. The standard for leadership is not the culture but the Word of God. There were very few women in primary leadership: Deborah was a prophetess and judge in the Old Testament. Priscilla was noted in the New Testament.

The influx of women in pastoral leadership is a cultural accommodation and worldly compromise. That is not a popular message. It is the truth. It is not a put-down on the power of a woman's service. God has designed ladies of grace for other kinds of ministries. If the Bible is God's blueprint, the people of God are going to be hard-pressed to find women pastors because there are none.

The ministry must always be set above the culture. The church is overrun with the foulest examples and the values of this world because of a lack of courage. But remember that the Bible was written by men who had courage to say "Thus saith the Lord" and to rebuke evil. So refuse to let carnal men rule the church, and resist any tolerance of error and immorality.

However, courage does not translate to tearing a church apart by a preacher's self-will or his dominant personality. Men of God are called to be humble.

And the servant of the Lord must not strive; but be gentle unto all men, apt to teach, patient, In meekness instructing those that oppose themselves; if God peradventure will give them repentance to the acknowledging of the truth; And that they may recover themselves out of the snare of the devil, who are taken captive by him at his will. (2 Timothy 2:24-26)

Courage is not only mandated for pastors but also for the people of God. How can men of God survive if the people do not stand up for what is right? So courage must be taught and exemplified.

When the people fail to be courageous, shepherds must determine whether to stand and rally people to the truth of the scriptures or to dust their feet off and go on to a people who will obey the Word. It is not a lack of courage if pastors leave because they don't have support. Rather, it is wisdom to save the witness of the church and not add to its division and strife.

The Man of God Leads in the Bible Way

Many churches in reality are not governed by pastors but by a family or group that dictates the terms at one point or the other. God cannot bless that, for it is not the church as he designed it. That kind of church is a club with no assurance of heaven. Too often, it can be a kind of hell on earth. A church void of biblical leadership, in whatever form it takes, is not true to the Lord.

God did not design the church to be governed by deacons who have the call to serve. The people of the Lord should not be ruled by those who give the most money. The Master never intended a majority rule. That is a European and American invention. There is little evidence of democracy in the early church. The people were governed by men of the Word and prayer (Acts 6:4).

The Lord Jesus warned us about the commandments of men usurping the commandments of God. It happened in his time, and it still clearly happens today. Following tradition is not all bad, but it can be damning while obeying the truth always saves.

May the Lord save the church from the politics of man and give grace to conform to the policies of God. Only then can the church evangelize and disciple as it should.

Men of God, be courageous enough to preach the truth in love, to bear witness of saving grace, to say, "Follow me as I follow Christ" (1 Corinthians 11:1). Stand against the devil in the church, and cherish every soul. God-called men should never coddle sin but confront it and warn of the judgment to come. Most of all, they fight to keep the Word exalted above the world in the church.

Summary Statements:

1. One of the best witnesses church leaders can have is to take immoral, unethical, and arrogant men out of the ministry and replace them with pure, true, and humble men of God.
2. There is one true interpretation of scripture; and the preacher should do all he can to proclaim it, regardless of the cost.
3. The ministry must always be set above the culture... Refuse to let carnal men rule the church, and resist any tolerance of error and immorality.
4. May the Lord save the church from the politics of man and give grace to conform to the policies of God. Only then can the church evangelize and disciple as it should.

Notes

How does church leadership qualify leaders without being guilty of judging their brothers as noted in Matthew 7:1-6?

The judgment that Christ speaks about there refers to hypocritical judgment when standards placed upon others are not applied to those who judge them. Leaders who qualify new leadership do so because those who make the call are serving the church as examples of the faith. Not all judgment is wrong—only self-righteous judgment. As Matthew 7:6 says, there are some who are not worthy of the pearls of the kingdom.

If a man of God leaves a church to preserve unity and prevent division, yet his departure is due to the people rejecting the truth of the Word of God, how does that protect the witness of the church?

Most evangelical churches are governed by majority rule—though it's a cultural value and not a biblical one. The pastor is called to preach the truth and also preserve unity. It is better to press on than to fight church politics. If he has godly men who will support him, he can take a stand and expose the ungodly.

How do men of God deal with carnality, error, and immorality in the church and not be guilty of "pulling up wheat along with the tares" as explained in Matthew 13:24–30?

The parable of Jesus does not teach that there is no place for church order and discipline. It teaches forbearance and perseverance. The unregenerate can have the appearance of true believers. It's not our place to pluck out pretenders from the church less those who know the Lord are also displaced. The angels will harvest at the end of the age. Yet the church must still uphold true doctrine, call for godly conduct, and do all discipline in love.

One part of scripture does not make another part of scripture null and void. Most of the New Testament epistles were written to correct, rebuke, and reprove behavior and belief of the churches. There were times when people were put out of the church, but it was done with humility and love (Galatians 6:1).

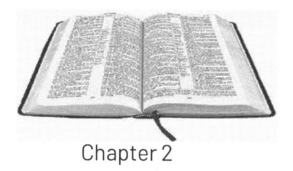

Chapter 2

The Word of God

One indispensable qualification for pastors is to know the Bible. Otherwise, there is no enduring ministry. Hebrews 4:12 has been quoted for generations.

For the word of God is quick, and powerful, and sharper than any two-edged sword, piercing even to the dividing asunder of soul and spirit, and of the joints and marrow, and is a discerner of the thoughts and intents of the heart.

Liberal theologians will say that the Bible contains the Word of God while Bible-believing preachers state firmly that it is the Word of God. Men of God must never dismiss the Word to justify inaction or give false comfort.

The context will reveal whether a verse is applicable or not. For example, the dietary laws were addressed by the Lord when Peter saw the conversion of Cornelius (Acts 10). Those who know God by his indwelling presence will learn how to interpret and obey the scriptures. As John 16:13 says, "When he, the Spirit of truth, is come, he will guide you into all truth..."

The Word of God is the Man of God 's Authority

In evangelical churches, the pulpit is in the center of the platform. It is not for the man of God who stands there, but for the book he preaches. It's the sacred desk which bears the sacred text. He preaches the very words of God. A true Bible church is never man-centered but

God-centered.

The words of the Lord are pure words: as silver tried in a furnace of earth, purified seven times. (Psalms 12:6)

Heaven and earth shall pass away, but my words shall not pass away. (Matthew 24:35)

What a powerful text in a chapter about the coming of the Lord! The verse from Matthew reminds us that the only authority men of God have to minister and do mission work is the scriptures. That means pastors must stay within the parameters of God's Word so that they do not accommodate the culture.

Authority speaks to power. The Bible is what the pastor preaches and lives. He is to appeal to the people through his own personal devotion to the Word and instruct them in the commands of Jesus. The Lord said heaven is for "he that doeth the will of my Father which is in heaven" (Matthew 7:21). The Bible is the church's moral and spiritual authority.

Every church must decide what their authority will be. Many prefer the culture and business models. Such churches have no moral authority because they have factored God out. That is why most churches do not exercise church discipline. In practice, they no longer believe that God still adheres to moral standards. They have compromised repeatedly until they are far from the truth of the Bible.

The Man of God Submits Himself to the Truth

Years ago, a seasoned pastor acknowledged that preachers were to submit to the Word of God and to lead their people to do the same. There is absolutely nothing to offer the world otherwise! Men who lead the church and love souls don't want to be guilty of what's said in 2 Timothy 3:7: "Ever learning, and never able to come to the knowledge of the truth." Truth that is received is obeyed.

Some men who have served the church have done some dastardly things: They have been guilty of sexual immorality and dishonesty with funds, and have fearlessly sacrificed the principles of the church for their monumental sense of pride. They have taught gross error and turned the sacred desk into a place of standup comedy. They have been winsome and charismatic yet spineless and compromising.

As a result, the culturally compromised church builds on sinking sand.

Therefore whosoever heareth these sayings of mine, and doeth them, I will liken him unto a wise man, which built his house upon a rock: And the rain descended, and the floods came, and the winds blew, and beat upon that house; and it fell not: for it was founded upon a rock. And every one that heareth these sayings of mine, and doeth them not, shall be likened unto a foolish man, which built his house upon the sand: And the rain descended, and the floods came, and the winds blew, and beat upon that house; and it fell: and great was the fall of it. (Matthew 7:24–27)

First Corinthians 3:11 says, "For other foundation can no man lay than that is laid, which is Jesus

Christ. Jesus is the solid rock. Winsome and charismatic personalities build on sinking sand; for if the church builds on men, they have no enduring witness or eternal worth. Men who pour their lives out between the pages of the Bible, on the other hand, are not those kinds of men.

> *Wherefore lay apart all filthiness and superfluity [excess] of naughtiness, and receive with meekness the engrafted word, which is able to save your souls. (James 1:21)*

The truth does not leave people the same. It examines hearts and motives. It purifies intents. It transforms souls.

The example of the man of God is crucial. He cannot lead the people of God to submit to the Bible's truth if he himself is not doing it. Pastors have to be what they expect all their members to be—soul-winning, disciple-making, people-loving, Bible-honoring, Holy Spirit-filled, zealous, joyful, overcoming souls—who get victory over sin.

The man of God brings his people to the Ten Commandments and shows them how to keep them by grace. He teaches the Great Commission of Jesus and organizes church and family life around it. He knows it is never enough to just believe by the Bible (James 2:19). He must bring the pages to life for the church and community.

The Man of God Rightly Interprets the Word of God

Second Timothy 2:15 is well known, but it's worth recalling it as the pastor's passion:

> *Study to shew thyself approved unto God, a workman*

Notes

9

that needeth not to be ashamed, rightly dividing the word of truth.

The New Testament word for approved means "to be tried." The man of God must be tried by his own message— so that his heart is sifted by the truth first. The phrase rightly divide is even more enlightening. It means "to be skillful and to correctly teach."

Here are a couple of examples from the Gospels. Matthew 18:20 is usually misinterpreted and misapplied.

> *For where two or three are gathered together in my*
> *name, there am I in the midst of them.*

This verse is applied to prayer when it really has very little to do with prayer!

The context in which Matthew 18 should be applied is church discipline—something that few churches do anymore. The Lord says that he will be with the church that deals with the people's sins. The intent there is not to pick-on a brother or sister but to correct a breach in their testimony— any conduct that brings reproach to the church. The Lord wants the church to protect its witness.

Luke 6:38 is another.

> *Give, and it shall be given unto you; good measure, pressed down, and*
> *shaken together, and running over, shall men give into your bosom. For*
> *with the same measure that ye mete withal it shall be measured to you*
> *again.*

Most preachers use that text to preach about giving though it has no application to giving but on forgiving. Read the verses around it.

The Man of God Leads the Bible Way

So here's how it works.

It is said that a "Christian" can commit sexual immorality, be a thief, teach what is false, and be an alcoholic but still go to heaven. These are just a few examples that been taught for generations. There is really no difference in conduct between a born-again believer and an unbeliever. But that is not the truth of the scriptures.

A careful study of the following verses will silence that form of libel against the Bible. It is the devil's doctrine to teach that believers can commit any sin and still be able to enter into heaven. Satan seeks to deceive and delude people into hell. Men of God must take the clear teaching of the scriptures above the degenerate and downgraded teaching of the age. Examine the clear truth of the following verses:

> *Know ye not that the unrighteous shall not inherit the kingdom of God?*

Be not deceived: neither fornicators, nor idolaters, nor adulterers, nor effeminate, nor abusers of themselves with mankind, Nor thieves, nor covetous, nor drunkards, nor revilers, nor extortioners, shall inherit the kingdom of God. And such were some of you: but ye are washed, but ye are sanctified, but ye are justified in the name of the Lord Jesus, and by the Spirit of our God. (1 Corinthians 6:9–11)

Now the works of the flesh are manifest, which are these; Adultery, fornication, uncleanness, lasciviousness [debauchery,riotous excess], Idolatry, witchcraft, hatred, variance [quarrels, contention, strife], emulations [envy, jealousy], wrath, strife, seditions, heresies, Envyings, murders, drunkenness, revelings, and such like: of the which I tell you before, as I have also told you in time past, that they which do such things shall not inherit the kingdom of God. (Galatians 5:19–21)

But fornication, and all uncleanness, or covetousness, let it not be once named among you, as becometh saints; Neither filthiness, nor foolish talking, nor jest- ing, which are not convenient [proper, fitting]: but rather giving of thanks. For this ye know, that no whoremonger,

Notes

11

*nor unclean person, nor covetous man, who is an idolater, hath any inheri-
tance in the kingdom of Christ and of God. (Ephesians 5:3–5)*

Those verses cover a lot of ground and describe the majority of church members! Many preachers and church members will not inherit the kingdom of heaven because they are guilty of the sins not as part of their past but as the makeup of their present. True repentance will mean putting these sins behind and pressing on for heaven.

So contrary to the church's present-day teaching, if you go to bed before you go to the altar (i.e., have premarital sex) and you do not repent (break free from your sins), you cannot be heaven bound. No unrepentant homosexual, thief, drunkard, partier, gossip, heretic, idolater—none of them—will be in heaven.

*Marriage is honourable in all, and the bed undefiled: but whoremongers
and adulterers God will judge. (Hebrews 13:4)*

Application of these verses may appear to be clear, but in light of the moral collapse of the church, the preacher is a voice crying in the wilderness with only a few who will listen. Many pastors have so watered down the Gospel that there is not much truth left. Many believe that a sinner's prayer secures eternal fire insurance so repentance is unnecessary. But that is not the Gospel.

The pure Gospel—interpreted and divided in the right way—defines salvation as obtaining victory over sin, hell, and the devil "by the blood of the Lamb, and by the word of their testimony" (Rev. 12:11). Anything else is another gospel—a false gospel, not a saving one.

The world and many in the church are crosscurrent with the truth. The Christian's lifestyle, however, must be altogether different.

Summary Statements:

How do believers get victory over sin?

1. The only authority men of God have to minister and do mission work is the scriptures.
2. Pastors have to be what they expect all their members to be—soul-winning, disciple-making, people- loving, Bible-honoring, Holy Spirit-filled, zealous, joyful, overcoming souls who get victory over sin.
3. The man of God must be tried by his own message—so that his heart is sifted by the truth first.
4. Men of God must take the clear teaching of the scriptures above the degenerate and downgraded teaching of the age.

*Walk in the light of the Lord, have fellowship with one another, and let the
blood of Jesus cleanse you from all sin...Confess your sins and know that
the Lord is faithful and just to forgive and to cleanse you from all unrighteous-
ness. (1 John 1:7, 9)*

What steps does the preacher take to properly interpret the Scripture?

He reads the context around the verses he has selected to preach and understands the times and generations in which they occur. He examines the words and their meanings. He lets the text speak for itself and compares it to similar passages.

Are the New Testament examples of immoral and unethical behaviors as found in 1 Corinthians 6:9–11, Galatians 5:19–21, and Ephesians 5:3–5 exhaustive and complete?

No, they are examples of ungodly conduct that reveal an absence of the Holy Spirit of God and the work of grace.

Notes

Chapter 3

How the Church Works

Most of the time, it doesn't. Most churches are not working because it is so hard to get anything done. Most ministries can barely be considered true because they are passive. For instance, one church took three years to accomplish a simple project. It was talked about, assignments were made, equipment was bought, but the finished product took over three years to get done.

Many times the people who are held responsible in the church do not have the real authority to make it happen.

Who directs the work of the church?

Is the purpose of the church to complete a series of projects or to work in partnership?

Is a worship service about entertainment or exalting Christ? Are disciples being made?

Are people being saved?

Is real mission work getting done?

Do decisions get made by those who are prayerful, Bible-guided, and fully informed?

Are opinions and politics more important than obedience and the practice of the Gospel?

Honest answers are unfortunately not forthcoming. When leaders really examine what is happening in most churches, they most likely will discover that what goes on is a far cry from what Jesus said the church should be about.

There appears to be a vacancy of excellence in the contemporary church. The standards for clubs are high, but the expectations in churches can be very low; a member or leader can behave or conduct themselves in unbelievable ways and still be in good standing. People inside and outside the church should be served with a strong work ethic and live out Christian character.

The Pastors Oversee the Work of the Church

The New Testament is clear in Acts and in Titus that the early church had a plurality of elders who directed the work. It is a worldly model when deacons serve as a board of directors and treat the pastor as the chief executive officer, who is subject to their criticism and directives. Such scenarios create an unreasonable setting where do-littles require much of one who is actually doing too much.

It is no better to have select families or businessmen make the decisions in a church. Most of the time, those who do are not spiritual people, have not paid the price of true ministry by being in the trenches, and they're not people of prayer.

Another broken model is when a pastor who has all the power is overpaid and dictates the terms of the fellowship causing grief to the Holy Spirit.

What about overbearing men of God?

Peter is clear that elders are not to be "lords over God's heritage" but "examples to the flock" (1 Peter 5:3). Leaders can have the tendency to be too dominant and guilty of power struggles. Pastors are indeed the elected and ordained leaders of the church; but they are not to stamp their image, name, and will all over the church.

The Lord protected the church from such broken models by designing a plurality of spiritual men to lead the church and oversee the work. These men, like the apostles, give themselves to prayer and the Word (Acts 6:4). They are not called to do all the visitation, go to every meeting, and be all things to all men as the only ministers in the church. All are called to the ministry.

The Pastors Give the Directives

How refreshing it would be to have churches that actually meet to worship and minister, not to vote and fight! It would be a revolutionary concept. There is absolutely no mandate in scripture to vote on anything and everything. A plurality of pastors in the New Testament made the decisions in the life of the church directed by the Word and guided by prayer.

The evidence of this can be seen in what was called the Jerusalem Council. In Acts 15:6, 13, 19, 22–23, the question of receiving Gentiles into the church was passionately deliberated. It was James, the brother of the Lord, chief elder in the Jerusalem church, who made the call. He did so with the approval of the apostles and elders. They were the authority of the early church.

Democracy in the church has brought about much division and strife, resulting in a terrible testimony in the

Notes

community where pastors have often been put on the road by unscrupulous and unspiritual people who do nothing to seek the lost and fulfill the Great Commission. Worse yet, by backroom politics, they betray and malign men of God who have little opportunity to defend their leadership. Politics and godly leadership simply do not mix.

The Pastors Oversee Church Discipline

The New Testament is full of actions that have been relegated to fossils and dinosaurs. That is, there are practices that the early church did that churches today are not willing to do. When was the last time that the people of God consulted Matthew 18:15-17 to deal with a brother or a sister at fault? How long has it been since a church exercised godly discipline over immorality?

Here are verses that evangelicals have disregarded and, in effect, cut out of their Bibles:

> *Now I beseech you, brethren, mark them which cause divisions and offences contrary to the doctrine which ye have learned; and avoid them. (Romans 16:17)*
>
> *But now I have written unto you not to keep company, if any man that is called a brother be a fornicator, or covetous, or an idolator, or a railer, or a drunkard, or an extortioner; with such an one no not to eat. (1 Corinthians 5:11)*
>
> *And have no fellowship with the unfruitful works of darkness, but rather reprove them. (Ephesians 5:11)*
>
> *A man that is an heretick after the first and second admonition reject; Knowing that he that is such is subverted, and sinneth, being condemned of himself. (Titus 3:10-11)*
>
> *If there come any unto you, and bring not this doctrine, receive him not into your house, neither bid him God speed: For he that biddeth him God speed is partaker of his evil deeds. (2 John 1:10-11)*

There are many more passages of that sort.

The New Testament is comprised of the Gospels, the Acts of the Holy Spirit, the Epistles and Revelation. The twenty-two books that follow Acts were written to keep the church from error and immorality. If the church fails to reprove, rebuke, and exhort, it has left the true Gospel.

Discipline is never to be done in condemnation, but it ought to be done to call people to life just as Galatians 6:1 says, "Brethren, if a man be overtaken in a fault, ye which are spiritual, restore such an one in the spirit of meekness; considering thyself, lest thou also be tempted."

The purpose of discipline is to save souls, to get them ready to stand before the Lord, and to help them see the church as heaven on earth.

16

People Go to Church to Worship and Minister

A church can only work if it has definitive leadership. The New Testament gives that charge to men of God whose authority is the Word of God and who are led by the Spirit of God. Church leadership should not be a tug-of-war and a constant delay of action because of revolts and demands of the people. Leaders are there to worship and minister, not to usurp and control.

The people of God suffer and become very regressive if there is not spiritual leadership as opposed to having political and worldly coalitions that govern the life and worship of the church. Part of the man of God's responsibility is to protect the church from dominant forces that would take the best of time, energy, and resources and give them over to lesser things.

In the place of worship, leadership must be resolved to get to God. Unending announcements and egotistical entertainment should have no place there. Godly leaders get people to God. Worship is not about programs wherein music and drama displace the Word and exhortation. When the church does worship—the people want to minister. The church works when every member ministers.

When an African warrior throws a spear, his precision is essential so that he hits the target. Churches today often miss the mark if the people are not being led to worship and to do ministry. The hunter can go out for hours and come back without meat. It is no different for the people of God when they go to church and come back empty and unfed.

Summary Statements:

1. All are called to the ministry.
2. A plurality of pastors in the New Testament made the decisions in the life o f the church.
3. The purpose of discipline is to save souls, to get them ready to stand before the Lord, and to help them see the church as heaven on earth.
4. When the church does worship—the people want to minister.

Notes

17

How can men of God lead yet not be seen as dictators?

Godly leadership can only come by submitting oneself to the Holy Spirit and following the example of Jesus. Shepherds are servant leaders. It is crucial to know that the Good Shepherd is the head of his church. Every pastor is an undershepherd. No man owns the church but the one who purchased it with his blood.

Is it really possible to have a church that is like heaven on earth?

Yes! The church that is full of the Holy Spirit and honors the Word of God will be like heaven on earth. It appears to be an unrealistic statement because churches are too busy fighting each other rather than fighting for souls. But when God's presence is manifested, nothing else matters but his mandates.

Chapter 4

The Great Commission

The Great Commission. This is what the church is on earth for, yet too many have zero activities and/ or real time directly connected to making disciples, teaching, applying biblical truth, and doing pure mission work. The first five books of the New Testament all have commissions from Jesus given in his last days on earth.

Go ye therefore, and teach all nations, baptizing them in the name of the Father, and of the Son, and of the Holy Ghost: Teaching them to observe all things whatsoever I have commanded you: and, lo, I am with you always, even unto the end of the world. Amen. (Matthew 28:19-20)

Go ye into all the world, and preach the Gospel to every creature. He that believeth and is baptized shall be saved; but he that believeth not shall be damned. (Mark 16:15-16)

And that repentance and remission of sins should be preached in his name among all nations, beginning at Jerusalem. And ye are witnesses of these things. (Luke 24:47–48)

Peace be unto you: as my Father hath sent me, even so send I you. (John 20:21)

But ye shall receive power, after that the Holy Ghost is come upon you: and ye shall be witnesses unto me both in Jerusalem, and in all Judaea, and in Samaria, and unto the uttermost part of the earth. (Acts 1:8)

How many congregations line up with the last will and testament of Jesus?

While Jesus gave the assignment to the local church, churches often exclude themselves and leave this work to mission agencies. Far too often, pastors are not favored if they seek to put the commission of Jesus into action. It is as if people are saying, "The Lord did not really mean what he said!" Remember, it was the serpent who first twisted the words of God when he said, "Ye shall not surely die" (Genesis 3:4). Satan still twists God's Word today.

What does a Great Commission church look like?

They make disciples. The people follow Jesus in very practical ways just as it's said in 1 John 2:6: "He that saith he abideth in him ought himself also so to walk, even as he walked." Such a people become witnesses just as the Gospels say, but most Christians do not share their faith. They fear man more than they fear God's command.

The obedient church teaches and applies biblical truth. That does not mean one has to fill up more notebooks with Bible knowledge, rather to do what Ephesians 4:15 pictures: "But speaking the truth in love, may grow up into him in all things, which is the head, even Christ..."True disciples, for example, forgive, speak in grace, and put away strife. Without such application, faith is void.

True disciples also do pure mission work. Much of what is done in the church is called missions even when they have no connection to what Jesus said. For example, sending young people to summer camp is not missions unless they learn to witness, get training in the Christian worldview and lifestyle, and get out among lost and needy people. Building projects, meeting needs, and community giveaways do not qualify as missions unless Jesus is shared.

The Great Commission of Jesus is the Command of the New Testament

The Great Commission is a reference to Matthew 28:19–20, but the other Gospels and Acts also echo the Master's mandate (if it is missed in the first Gospel). The people of God have a limited amount of emotional energy and time. When scarce resources are spent on meetings without a plan of action, then the priorities of the Lord for his church are ignored.

If Christians are not making disciples, growing in faith, and working in missions, they are playing church and failing to be the church. There are many "good things" that occupy believers' time and zap their energy; but if they refuse to do what the Master says, then the world becomes a hard taskmaster, and the culture—and not scripture—sets the standard.

One heart-stopping verse is found in Matthew 7:21:

> Not every one that saith unto me, Lord, Lord, shall enter into the kingdom of heaven; but he that doeth the will of my Father which is in heaven.

There is also the potent truth of James 1:22:

> But be ye doers of the word, and not hearers only, deceiving your own selves.

There's another worth reading, and it's in the final chapter of the Bible:

> Blessed are they that do his commandments, that they may have right to the tree of life, and may enter in through the gates into the city. (Revelation 22:14)

Time is short, so if a church is unwilling to do the commands of Jesus, obedient believers must go to one that will!

The Great Commission Calls All to Make Disciples

The New Testament church multiplied disciples. They were witnesses who poured out their lives into people. When the people strayed, the apostles wrote to the churches to bring correction and call them back to the apostolic teaching. The church is built on the foundation of such revolutionary teaching (Ephesians 2:20).

It was revolutionary because it required self-denial, forward action, and Gospel zeal. The New Testament

Notes

21

word was disciple, not believer. Today, we have just believers. Belief is not the point, but rather it is growing in grace to know Christ and make him known.

> *Thou believest that there is one God; thou doest well;*
> *the devils also believe, and tremble. (James 2:19)*

How do we "make disciples"? The old line churches used to teach catechism! That makes most evangelicals uncomfortable, but there is much worth and value in teaching historic Christian doctrine. What is essential is to teach biblical truth and a Christian worldview at every age level so that children, youth, and adults know the Word and learn to obey it.

But it involves more than just learning—there's also doing the Christian disciplines like prayer, fasting, reading, applying the Bible, growing confident in sharing the faith, and having a proper reverence for God in daily life. Making disciples will mean that the church has the kind of environment to reproduce the Christian life that we read about in the New Testament in Acts 2:42, 46-47:

> *And they continued steadfastly in the apostles' doctrine and fellowship,*
> *and in breaking of bread, and in prayers...And they, continuing daily with*
> *one accord in the temple, and breaking bread from house to house, did eat*
> *their meat with gladness and singleness of heart, Praising God, and hav-*
> *ing favour with all the people. And the Lord added to the church daily such*
> *as should be saved.*

The Great Commission Takes the Church to the Ends of the Earth

If the local church fails to get the people out of the classroom and sanctuary, then it is not a Great Commission church. Historic Christian faith that is taught and obeyed will carry Christians to the streets, prisons, homes, hospitals, and unreached regions around the world.

Consider the heart of the apostle Paul in Romans 1:5;16:26:

> *By whom we have received grace and apostleship, for obedience to the*
> *faith among all nations, for his name...But now is made manifest, and by*
> *the scriptures of the prophets, according to the commandment of the*
> *everlasting God, made known to all nations for the obedience of the faith...*

The apostles had one goal, and that was obedience of the faith for all nations. It is an impossible task if the gospel that is prescribed demands little—is a come-and-see message and not a go-and-tell mandate—and then utilizes all the church's resources for personal comfort. That is unlike the Gospel of the apostles—which demanded much, mobilized the church house to house, and spent the early church's resources to the max as the people set aside their comfort.

Can anyone imagine the church governed by the apostles having hundreds of thousands of dollars sitting in a bank collecting interest? How about having budgets where 90 percent of the funds went to staff that did little to fulfi ll the Great Commission and to pay for maintenance costs of buildings that were dedicated to fun and games, big feeds, and social activities void of soul-winning and disciple-making action?

If devoted Christians were to compare the church of today with that which Jesus founded, it would be like night and day—a far cry from his intention. The church of the apostles had less and did much more. Churches today take pride in their mini empires, but they've forsaken the kingdom of God. Too many believe there is more need at home than there is where the Gospel is unknown.

Spiritual Leadership Commits to Local and Global Evangelism and Missions

When the constrast between the action of the church in the pages of scripture is compared to the inaction in the church today, there is a strong case for apostasy. The church of our time has too often downgraded obedience (in most cases, to the point of nonexistent obedience) to the Lord for the strong opinions of men. Men have extolled politics and business in the church to displace God's power and blessing. The Holy Spirit is absent in many services, and only a few have noticed.

The church can only recover when they come to grips with the Great Commission and understand that it is the command of heaven. It is the very call of God to make disciples and pay the cost to take the Gospel to the ends of the earth. Then the assurance of his presence will be with his people wherever they go. The church is so much more than a social club hell-bent on comfort and convenience!

What can be done to get the people of God back to the Great Commission?

Evangelism and missions must have more funds than food and flowers in the church. Youth ministry must be more than pizza and amusement parks. Children's activities have to move beyond bounce houses and balloons. The spiritual revolution must come first to church leaders and parents.

Every pastor and staff minister should personally be committed to local and global evangelism and missions. There should be no deacon elected in a

Notes

church that is unwilling to give and go for the Gospel cause. Those who have not seen that the worship of Revelation includes all peoples and nations should not lead worship. The passion of the church that honors Jesus will be missions.

Most will honestly say, "It is not my thing." If that is an honest assessment, then the world must be displaced in such hearts—because it is the "Lord's thing." The Great Commission was the Master's last instructions. He knew men were thick-headed and hard hearted, so he strategically placed it in the last chapters of every Gospel and the first chapter of Acts. It is time to get it and go!

Summary Statements:

1. Time is short, so if a church is unwilling to do the commands of Jesus, obedient believers must go to one that will!
2. What is essential is to teach biblical truth and a Christian worldview at every age level so that children, youth, and adults know the Word and learn to obey to it.
3. Historic Christian faith which is taught and obeyed will carry Christians to the streets, prisons, homes, hospitals, and unreached regions around the world.
4. The passion of the church that honors Jesus will be missions.

What is historic Christian faith?

It is Bible teaching that has come from Christ and the apostles through the ages—one that stands apart from the traditions of men. It affirms the trinity, the virgin birth, the deity of Christ, the bodily resurrection of Jesus, the evangelical and missionary nature of the church, and the return of the Lord for his church.

The traditions of men add to what Jesus and the apostles taught. Often, men place their traditions on equal footing with the truth of scripture. It is alarming how much is done in the church that has no foundation in the scriptures.

Are not all Christians missionaries and all Christian action missions?

No, they're not in practice. Christians do not defi ne missions. Missions defi ne Christians. They're not missionaries if they do not share Jesus. It's not missions if evangelism and discipleship are not done. The distinguishing mark of an apostolic faith is going, teaching, and baptizing.

Chapter 5

The Priority of Prayer

A faithful prayer life takes discipline and hard choices. Spiritual leaders have to decide it is worth it to check out of the activity and demands of the day to spend time with God, to be still and know him (Psalms 46:10). Unfortunately, leaders can know much about prayer, but not put it into practice. Prayer may be the hardest work of the Christian's life and ministry.

All believers need those times of personal worship. It is not a matter of just reading a few chapters in the Bible and whispering a prayer, but giving oneself to the kind of prayer that pours out of the heart until it is empty before God and then filled again with his presence. Such a life of prayer is evident in Nehemiah, the Psalms of David (expressly), and the Gospel of Mark (Mark 1:35).

In the history of the church, there have been men who have written about prayer from their practice (e.g., E.M. Bounds, Andrew Murray, and Leonard Ravenhill). Books by any of these knee-calloused preachers are bound to inspire and, at the same time, convict the reader. Prayer was something that the Lord spent much of his time doing, and it is his present work in heaven.

Personal Testimony about Prayer

When I was eighteen years old and a freshman at Oklahoma Baptist University, my roommate asked if

Notes

25

I wanted to "tarry" with him for a night. I had no idea what he was talking about. We went out by a lake and prayed all night. I was finished by midnight though I did manage a few more words when the stars began to fade, but he prayed throughout the night until the sun reflected upon the lake.

That night changed my perspective on prayer. In later years, we had Friday night prayer meetings in West Virginia at the church where I served as pastor. We started at 9:00 p.m. and prayed until we finished (usually around 1:00-2:00 a.m.). There were about four or five of us most of the time.

The presence of the Lord bathed that sanctuary and altar. When we finished praying, we always wanted more.

Churches Are to Be Houses of Prayer

If the church is going to be a house of prayer for all people and all nations as Isaiah 56:7 and Mark 11:17 says, the people must be at home with prayer. The truth is very few pastors are comfortable with heartfelt prayer, much less the rest of the people. This is not the ritual of prayer but the reality of seeking God for his presence and his power in ministry—and more importantly, to know him all the more.

Prayer opens doors to people's hearts in the community. In general, people like to be prayed for. There are a few exceptions (but those hearts are stone cold). Men of God hear hundreds of times, "Pastor, remember to pray for me!" Every class should be a prayer band. Children and youth should be taught to pray. Families ought to pray together, but it will not work if those prayers are lifeless.

The kinds of prayers the church is to pray are described in 1 Timothy 2:1-4—supplications (begging and pleading), intercessions (petition on behalf of another), giving of thanks, prayers for authorities and rulers, and pleas for salvation. The effectual work of the church and effective communication of the truth depend on the atmosphere of prayer.

The image of scripture is the people of God praying for the nations. What a difference it would make if Christians could see nations becoming God-fearing and placing value on souls because every church house was a place of prayer! Churches are known for being political bases much more than prayer centers. Spirit-filled believers know that prayer is a formidable weapon against a sinful culture.

Churches that pray for nations are more apt to send their people to those nations in need of the Gospel. Each nation should have people of faith interceding for them. Revelation verses 5:9 and 7:9 show that people from every nation will be before the throne in heaven. There are 196 nations (independent countries) on earth, and all of them need a viable Gospel witness and Bible churches.

The Church is to Be a Place of intercession

Verses 26 and 34 in Romans Chapter 8 reveal that the work of the Holy Spirit in the heart of believers and the Son at the right hand of the throne is...intercession! That means praying for others by taking on their burdens, trials, and pain. The Spirit of God does that work in believers as they see the lost world and the struggling church. The Lord Jesus intercedes. It is his primary work until the Father sends him back to earth.

Likewise the Spirit also helpeth our infirmities: for we know not what we should pray for as we ought: but the Spirit itself maketh intercession for us with groanings that cannot be uttered. (Romans 8:26)

Romans 8:26 shows the compassion of Spirit-filled disciples. The verse gives an honest assessment of spiritual ineptness without the Holy Spirit, but with him, prayers and supplications and intercessions pour forth. The spirit groans with words that cannot be spoken. That is not a reference to speaking in tongues—for the words are not spoken—but prevailing prayer.

Who is he that condemneth? It is Christ that died, yea rather, that is risen again, who is even at the right hand of God, Who also maketh intercession for us. (Romans 8:34)

Romans 8:34 is set in heaven, where Jesus cries out for his church. He is praying! He is interceding for his people! Hebrews 7:25 confirms this work.

Wherefore he is able also to save them to the uttermost that come unto God by him, seeing he ever liveth to make intercession for them.

If Christian leaders are to be like Christ, they must pray as he does.

Christians grossly neglect prayer. If they do pray, it is often for gaining personal blessings and not for building the kingdom. Prayer appears very real when people offer them up for their errant or hurting children. Tears flow, hearts are broken, and they are not ashamed to ask for prayer for their babies. Yet that is where it stops.

In the scripture, in times of great crisis, fasting was coupled with prayer. For many parents, fasting is too much to ask. What did Jesus say in Matthew 17:21 when he came down from the mount of transfiguration? He said, "Howbeit this kind goeth not out but by prayer and fasting." There is a divine dynamic in fasting that denies the flesh and stretches the soul to give heartfelt petition.

Notes

The Church is Where Prayers are Answered!

John's Gospel has some remarkable references that the church no longer believes in. They are pure dynamite for the people of God when they see prayer as something God intends to answer.

> *Ask, and it shall be given you; seek, and ye shall find; knock, and it shall be opened unto you; For every one that asketh receiveth; and he that seeketh findeth; and to him that knocketh it shall be opened. (Matthew 7:7–8)*

The people of God seem so used to unanswered prayer because of disbelief or some disconnection between the request and meeting of needs.

But to the contrary, God often answers prayers, yet there is little or no thanks in return. The truth is most believers are frustrated with prayer because it is not on their terms. People should keep in mind that prayers are subject to God's timing, will, and answers. As spiritual leaders read through the Gospels, they see how big prayer was for the Master and the apostles. Then there's the repeated promise in the Gospel of John:

> *And whatsoever ye shall ask in my name, that will I do, that the Father may be glorified in the Son. If ye shall ask any thing in my name, I will do it. (John 14:13–14)*

> *If ye abide in me, and my words abide in you, ye shall ask what ye will, and it shall be done unto you. (John 15:7)*

> *And in that day ye shall ask me nothing. Verily, verily, I say unto you, What-soever ye shall ask the Father in my name, he will give it you. Hitherto have ye asked nothing in my name: ask, and ye shall receive, that your joy may be full. (John 16:23–24)*

Do you think the Master meant it? He tells his disciples to ask in three back-to-back chapters in the last Gospel. The condition is that they abide in him and ask in his name—that is, in his character and purposes. The fruit of answered prayer is joy! Oh, how the church needs joy— the joy of answered prayer! With this thought, the voice of Isaiah comes to mind:

> *Behold, the Lord's hand is not shortened, that it cannot save; neither is his ear heavy, that it cannot hear: But your iniquities have separated be-tween you and your God, and your sins have hid his face from you, that he will not hear. (Isaiah 59:1–2)*

There is a big problem with sin in the church—often, the sin of prayerlessness. Men of God cannot see the face of God unless they seek him.

> *When Thou saidst, Seek ye my face; my heart said unto thee, Thy face, Lord, will I seek. (Psalms 27:8)*

This must be the generation that seeks the Lord's face and receives his blessing (Psalms 24:6).

What does it mean to seek the face of God to get answers, to take care of sin, to know that God hears and will work?

It means time in prayer, worship, and waiting. It includes the motivation to pray with others and to have the knowledge that the heavens are not brass. It is elevating prayer above other activities and priorities that have no biblical foundation. It is to bend the knee and be like Jesus.

Heaven Helps, and Hell Fights a Praying Church

If the church house would be first a prayer house for all people and nations, there would be power to save and resources to minister, and the folly of division and self-will would be burned away. If only men and women of prayer were permitted to lead the church, then most of the worldliness and carnality would be washed away quickly.

Men would begin to intercede for their wives and wives for their husbands, and marriages would get stronger. Children would be the targets of prayer and fasting at every stage of development, and the devil would not have his way with them. Men of God would have the church praying for them rather than fighting their ministries. Prayer would make for a new day in the church.

Prayers would be answered, and the church would be full of believers rather than unbelievers. (There are times when there are honestly more unbelievers than believers running the church). Joy would be the chief character of the people of God rather than cynicism and judgmental tones. It would be refreshing to know that prayer was real.

Prayer is a funny thing: it does not work if it is not exercised. No one can fool heaven or hell. They know whether or not they have a praying church. Heaven helps it and hell fights it. The people of God understand spiritual opposition, and they recognize it for what it is. Still, they

Notes

29

pray through it all. Heaven comes down because the Spirit of God is unhindered in the house of God.

Without prayer, there are no "turbo engines" and "jet power" for the church. Instead, the people of God are relegated back to mule skinning (term for riding wagons pulled by mules) and it is not a pleasant task.

Without prayer, the church is powerless and pitiful, and the same goes for the preachers and leaders who seek to do God's work. Christlikeness requires men and women of faith to step aside, pray, grip the mercy seat, and intercede.

Summary Statements:

1. The effectual work of the church and effective communication of the truth depend on the atmosphere of prayer.
2. If Christian leaders are to be like Christ, they must pray as he does.
3. The church needs the joy of answered prayer.
4. If only men and women of prayer were permitted to lead the church, then most of the worldliness and carnality would be washed away quickly.

Why do churches neglect prayer?

For the same reason Christians do. It takes time and discipline to pray. It requires shutting out the world and the list of demands and things to do. Investment in prayer is prompted by the conviction that God can do more than man can. Like so much of the Christian life, there is a mile-wide gap between what is known and how it is to be lived out. All believers struggle with narrowing that gap and boosting the life of faith.

What does a church of prayer look like?

The first thing that stands out is evidence of the presence of God and a high degree of God-dependence. The leaders are marked by prayer in the totality of their ministry. The people are prayed over and the community knows it. There is consistent prayer for the nations to hear the glad tidings. Ministries of the church are bathed in prayer. The more the church is known for prayer, the greater the Gospel ministry.

Chapter 6

The Work of the Holy Spirit

Without the work of the Holy Spirit in the church, there is no regeneration, conviction, or gifting. That is where far too many churches are today—void of the Holy Spirit and operating in the flesh. In fact, churches have grieved the Spirit of God due to the inability to forgive, revolt against the Word, rebellion against pastoral leadership, and disservice to the people of God. It breaks God's heart when there's an unwillingness to evangelize, make disciples, and do mission service.

Churches are also guilty of quenching the Spirit of God by "throwing cold water" on any sign of zeal for the Gospel, obedience to the faith, and respect for the wisdom of God above the foolishness of men. The church is impotent with inaction and a lack of spiritual progress without the power of the Holy Spirit. When the Spirit of God is present, everything changes. Acts 5:32 reveals the crux of having a church charged with the presence of the Holy Spirit:

> *And we are witnesses of these things; and so is also the Holy Ghost, whom God hath given to them that obey him.*

Worship is all about God saturating the atmosphere, shaking and shaping hearts. He is there when his people obey him.

Notes

31

Too much is done without the Holy Spirit. Way too much is done only in the flesh. It leaves people in ministry with a sense of hopelessness. Therefore, the church must get back to the source of power and blessing.

Now the God of hope fill you with all joy and peace in believing, that ye may abound in hope, through the power of the Holy Ghost. (Romans 15:13)

Most believers in the church are not Spirit-filled. That is not a reference to having a particular spiritual gift but to living in such a way that God governs the soul and directs Christian service. When God's people are Spirit-filled, they are humble, content, and pure in heart. They have a burden for souls and to be used by God to encourage and evangelize others. Spirit-filled people are prayerful people, and they're always ready to minister to those in need.

The void in the church is not so much the lack of resources and the need for more people to work for the Master. It is not even the saving of souls and teaching men the commands of Jesus. It is not going for more harmony and greater faith. It is the work of the Holy Spirit. When God's presence is not in the company of the redeemed, then there is no power over the enemy, nor will there be any means of salvation. The Spirit of God is the one person the church cannot do without!

Do Not Grieve the Spirit of God

Ephesians 4:30 says, "And grieve not the Holy Spirit of God, whereby ye are sealed unto the day of redemption." The context reveals what grieves the Spirit of God: corrupt communication, bitterness, wrath, anger, clamor, evil speaking, malice, and the inability to forgive. The church is riddled with these sins, and there are those in church leadership who represent these devilish traits. They have "a form of godliness" but "deny the power thereof" (2 Timothy 3:5).

Sins of the tongue grieve the Spirit of God, who has sealed believers until the day of redemption. He has sealed them, so he will never leave them. Yet they dishonor him when they engage in corrupt communication (speak bad and rotten words) in bitterness, anger, or malice and with clamor (loud and contentious) and evil, or an unwillingness to forgive. All of these grieve the Spirit of God. If people know and love him, they will not go on speaking like the devil.

The people of God can be so easily taken in by people who say they know the Lord but speak the devil's language. Jesus confronted the Jewish leaders of his day and exposed them as liars and murderers (John 8:43–47) because they were motivated by deceit and hate. Christian leaders can be sure that if that's the mode of operation for troublemakers in the church, they are pretenders. Jesus said that people will be known by their fruits (Matthew 7:20).

Tattlers and busybodies, along with gainsayers, are not the servants of the Lord. Make no mistake. Those who cannot control their tongues are just as James said: they have hearts that are full of deadly poison (James 3:8). In James 3:6, it says that the tongue is "a world of iniquity," that it can "defileth the whole body, and setteth on fire the course of nature; and it is set on the fire of hell." No man can tame it! The tongue is an "unruly evil." Nothing and no one is able to tame the tongue but the Holy Spirit.

Do Not Quench the Spirit of God

First Thessalonians 5:19 has this admonition: "Quench not the Spirit." The context is found in a very practical passage about how to live the Christian life (1 Thessalonians 5:12-24). A literal rendering would read, "Don't put out the fire of the Holy Spirit." That does not mean that anything and everything can go on in the church as long as the Spirit of God gets the (for lack of a better word) blame. Many so-called Christian leaders blame God for their own irreverence and blasphemy.

Christians can only know for sure what God has said when they read the Word, not from the outrageous claims of men. The inspiration behind the prophets and apostles who produced the Bible is no longer available. No impression can match that level of inspiration though many may say otherwise. Men and women "quench the Spirit" when they add to the Word or seek to equate what men say with the same authority as what God said.

The fire of God is put out in the church when there is partiality.

> "But if ye have respect to persons, ye commit sin, and are convinced of the law as transgressors. (James 2:9)

The New Testament church is open to all members who live a life of repentance—regardless of race, class, or background. The apostle Paul listed lifestyles believers came from in 1 Corinthians 6:9-11. (Then he adds those wonderful words "And such were some of you...")

The Spirit of God is quenched when God's people refuse to obey the truth and respond to conviction of sin. Stubborn pride, the fear of man, and secret sins keep many believers in a perpetual state of lukewarm devotion. The result of not so-called Christian leaders blame God for their own irreverence and blasphemy.

> "But if ye have respect to persons, ye commit sin, and are convinced of the law as transgressors. (James 2:9)

Notes

33

The Spirit of God is quenched when God's people refuse to obey the truth and respond to conviction of sin. Stubborn pride, the fear of man, and secret sins keep many believers in a perpetual state of lukewarm devotion. The result of not obeying the Spirit is living life in a pile of ashes where the fire once burned bright but has only a few coals left.

Keep being filled with the Spirit!

Ephesians 5:18 says, "And be not drunk with wine, wherein is excess; but be filled with the Spirit." That is, "keep being filled and controlled" by the Spirit. The Bible teaches us that believers are baptized by the Holy Spirit once when they are regenerated and come to saving grace, but they are repeatedly filled with the Holy Spirit—and need to be.

Drunkards are often unashamed of their drinking habits. They will spend and be spent to taste that rat poison. They will sacrifice family, income, and reputation. Should not believers have the same willingness to be filled with the Spirit? The difference will be that Spirit-filled Christians will be devoted to their families and be good stewards of their income.

These are the "excesses" of the Christian life: sharing the faith with all kinds of people, living by the truth of the Bible, serving the forsaken and forgotten, and being strong in the Lord in the spiritual battle against Satan. When believers are filled with the Spirit of God, they are unashamed of his wonderful grace and his good work.

God wants all that call on the name of the Lord to live for him in practical ways. Romans 8 is the place to go to determine whether a life is being lived in the flesh or by the Spirit:

1. Spirit-filled Christians will have life and peace (Romans 8:6).
2. They do not live for the flesh, but put to death the deeds of the flesh (Romans 8:13).
3. The Spirit of God leads and directs all true believers (Romans 8:14).
4. They know they are the children of God by the witness of the Spirit (Romans 8:16).
5. The Spirit makes them "heirs of God, and joint-heirs with Christ" (Romans 8:17).
6. He intercedes on behalf of all believers (Romans 8:26–27).
7. Spirit-filled believers are more than conquerors (Romans 8:37).
8. No matter what, nothing can separate them from the love of God (Romans 8:39).

The Spirit of God increases boldness because he loads up believers with grace and gifts to serve. When unction is missing, he may be missing!

> *Now if any man have not the Spirit of Christ, he is*
> *none of his. (Romans 8:9)*

Romans 12 reveals how a Spirit-filled Christian acts in this world of trouble and temptation:

1. As a living sacrifice not conformed to this world doing God's will (Romans 12:1–2).
2. Humble, preferring others, condescending to the lowly (Romans 12:3, 10, 16).
3. Gifted by the Holy Spirit, as he determines, to serve the church (Romans 12:4–8).
4. Loving without hypocrisy, hating evil, cleaving to the good (Romans 12:9).
5. Not lazy, fervent in spirit, and always serving the Lord (Romans 12:11).
6. Ever rejoicing in hope, patient in tribulation, and instant in prayer (Romans 12:12).

7. Meeting the needs of the saints and given to hospitality (Romans 12:13).
8. Blessing persecutors, not recompensing evil or avenging (Romans 12:14, 17, 19).
9. Rejoicing for the glad hearted and weeping with the brokenhearted (Romans 12:15).
10. Honest in the sight of all men and living at peace with all men (Romans 12:17-18).
11. Feeding their enemies, giving them drink, and meeting their needs (Romans 12:20).
12. Not being overcome by evil but overcoming evil with good (Romans 12:21).

The only way Christians can be filled with the Spirit is to live contrary to the world. So many believe they are Spirit-filled, but if they are not a match to what's described in Romans 8 and 12, they're not!

As previously noted, the Word of God is the only standard—not culture or a religious movement.

Do Not Resist the Spirit of God

There is an additional hindrance to the work of the Holy Spirit seen in the church—that is resisting the work of the Spirit. The pinnacle of Stephen's preaching before his death by stoning is found in Acts 7:51. "Ye stiffnecked and uncircumcised in heart and ears, ye do always resist the Holy Ghost: as your father did, so do ye." Just after that statement, they proved his premise by stopping up their ears and refusing to hear him who was filled with the Spirit.

Indeed, the Jews had a long history of resisting the prophets and the Word of God. It cost them dearly: a divided kingdom, exile, Gentile domination and repeated national judgments. The church is little different in division, exile, worldly domination and judgment because we often love tradition more than truth and ceremony more than worship. Churches may be in a fallen state because they resist God like the Hebrews did in the wilderness in spite of the evidence of the wonders of God.

Notes

The ways of God with man are a wonder, but a greater wonder is the persistent resistance to believe, to be thankful and obey among the people that say they believe. The Gentiles in the days of the Exodus showed greater faith than the Hebrews, just as the world may have greater faith in the God of the Bible than believers do today! The hindrance to saving faith is not the ability of God. It is the inability of believers to act on faith. Passive faith is disobedience and disregard for the commands of God.

In Stephen's day, they rejected his interpretation of Jewish history because it exposed their disobedience to the Law of God and lack of contrition over their own sinfulness. It made them angry—so angry that they broke the Law of God with murder in their hearts and blood on their hands. Their religion killed the true messenger and their rage silenced the truth in their ears. This scene has been played out over and over again throughout the ages as men ignore the truth.

These points of resistance keep the church sliding back, standing still or shriveling up from spiritual vitality and victory:

1. Christian leaders still carry their titles and fill the offices without making disciples.
2. Missionaries and Christian workers often exempt themselves from serving in the local church.
3. We suffer hearing loss: The Lord requires us to give ten percent plus and we give two percent or less.
4. The Lord has the world on His heart to search and rescue. We have the world on our minds to pacify.
5. He calls us to be sanctified and transformed, but many in the church are carnal and conformed.
6. The Bible reveals giving by obedience and sacrifice while we raise funds and make sales appeals.
7. We read in the Acts where believers added and multiplied but today we see subtraction and division.
8. The Word prioritizes the spiritual and eternal. We have traded them for the material and temporary.
9. Pastors have become entrepreneurs, coaches and chief executive officers, no longer men of God.
10. We bombard one man with the Gospel and completely neglect another man with no witness at all.
11. Poor spiritual health goes back to gross negligence and empty prayer lives. The fire of God must fall!
12. Gospel work will advance in abundant fruitfulness when we humble ourselves before the Living God.

James 4:17 says,

> "Therefore to him that knoweth to do good, and doeth it not, to him it is sin." That is where many in the church are today, including shepherds. We resist the commands of God for a lost world and fail to train and mobilize the church with a lively faith. Small wonder people feel defeated.

Church activity can easily be reduced down to sharing tasty meals, choir practice, a few special events a year and church trips while discipleship, prayer, and personal witness are go unscheduled.

The obedient church resists the world, dismisses excuses, does what God says and spiritually thrives. They do not stop their ears—they open their eyes to what God is doing. When believers resist the Spirit of God, they shut up the windows of heaven. Works of grace stop or become a trickle and the church stumbles along in the flesh. It is not a good place to be. We do not want to wander in the wilderness, but cross over the Jordan into the Promise Land.

Spiritual Leaders are Full of the Spirit of God

Spirit-filled Christians are as rare now as they were then in biblical times. What are the identifying marks of Spirit-filled people? They do not grieve the Spirit of God by the way they speak of others. There are some things they will speak of and other things they won't. They will speak of the glad tidings, not evil. They are not gossips but gospelers. What would the church be like if it were empty of gossips and full of people who shared the Gospel?

They do not put out the fire of the Spirit of God in saving grace, conviction of sin, and true times of worship. They are not wet blankets and can't-do church members. They are encouragers and exhorters. They come along, help the weak, and bless the downhearted. The Spirit-filled will sacrifice while others seek comfort. They will bless the men of God and ladies of grace who serve so faithfully. Spirit-filled believers are not up and down, in and out, on fire one minute and as cold as ice the next. They are always full of the Spirit of grace and supplication.

Acts 6:3 records a time when the early church sought to meet the needs of neglected widows and find men to serve them. These men are seen as the early deacons.

> *Wherefore, brethren, look ye out among you seven men of honest report, full of the Holy Ghost and wisdom, whom we may appoint over this business.*

How many deacons are "full of the Holy Ghost and wisdom"?

That should be the qualifier for any deacon or pastor in the church. The church today looks for worldly qualifications and, consequently, pays a dear price for it. Only spiritual leadership can do the work of the church

Notes

because the word for church literally means "to be called out" from the world. The person and the work of the Holy Spirit is the greatest witness a church and spiritual leaders can have!

Summary Statements:

1. The people of God can be so easily taken in by people who say they know the Lord, but speak only the devil's language.
2. The Spirit of God is quenched when God's people refuse to obey the truth or to respond to the conviction of the Holy Spirit.
3. The only way Christians can be filled with the Spirit is to live contrary to the world.
4. Spirit-filled believers are not up and down, in and out, on fire one minute and as cold as ice the next.

Do Spirit-filled believers suffer from depression to the point where they have a cold heart?

Christians can suffer from depression and be coldhearted. But not Spirit-filled Christians. The New Testament never shows a Spirit-filled believer as downcast. Such a condition is evidence of the need for "refilling." The Spirit of God will bring victory and overcoming power.

What further steps can one take to be filled with the Spirit and to live contrary to the world?

The starting place is an open Bible and a readiness to pour the heart out in prayer. Doing practical ministry like outreach evangelism, encouraging others, and staying faithful to times of worship all help in nurturing spiritual life. Most of all, be cleansed of all known sin.

Chapter 7

True Worship

Christian leaders have a paramount challenge when it comes to worship. All around the globe, there have been worship wars on the styles of music. At times, music ministers may have greater affection for entertainment than actual faithful Bible preaching. Prayers can be dry as dust and not fitted for public worship. Bible reading may be dull and without inflection. Announcements are very seldom Godward.

Worship is really not about the choir or the children or the preacher. It is about the Almighty, the glory of God, and giving people the opportunity to meet the Lord in an unforgettable way. Worship is not something to be endured as a timed event, but it is to be enjoyed in the very presence of the Lord and his people. True worship happens when people make time for God.

Most services never get to God. Whenever worship services highlight the accomplishments of men above the honor of God, there is failure to worship him. Too often speakers are given long introductions. No true man of God would be happy about this. First Corinthians 1:29,31 says, "That no flesh should glory in his presence... he that glorieth, let him glory in the Lord."

One of the worst "worship zappers" are the announcements. A rousing song is sung to call the people to worship, and then announcements follow. Even if they are given at the end of a service, they are a downer.

39

People do not worship during announcements! Yes, the church needs to be informed. However, church leaders can share announcements in a variety of other ways, but they should preserve the worship time for worship.

The Gospel invitation should be the highpoint of the service, yet many people cut out to go to the bathroom or take an early exit by that time. A well-managed service will make the invitation a time for prayer at the altar, personal application of the message, and quiet moments for reflection. It should not be tacked on at the end of the service. It is as a time to get before God.

Priming the Pump of Worship

There are a variety of views on how worship should work.

What are the essential components of worship? Who should get the most time in the one to two hours scheduled? There are at least three events to get ready for worship: prayer, Bible reading, and singing. Worship is not a performance. It's a public service to direct people to God. Worship should always be done with excellence and earnestness for the audience of just One.

How about prayer?

Prayer can be just an honored ritual. It can be bone dry. What is needed are heartfelt prayers mixed with unyielding faith. Some prayers start out slow then catch fire, and then it's over before the observer knows it. The rise in emotion is predictable, and the end is forced. God alone discerns the sincerity of any prayer, but prayer is for his ears, not men's.

Prayer cannot be a show. It is our means of communication with the Lord. A great example is found in Acts 4:24–30, where the apostles prayed. The result is in Acts 4:31:

> *And when they had prayed, the place was shaken where they were assembled together; and they were all filled with the Holy Ghost, and they spake the Word of God with boldness.*

Reading the scriptures prepares hearts for worship. These components are not void of worship by any means. They bring the people of God to the place where they can open up their hearts before him. Paul instructs Timothy, "Till I come, give attendance to reading, to exhortation, to doctrine" (1 Timothy 4:13). The Bible should be read with inflection and inspiration. How about singing? It dominates many church services and can trump Bible preaching. What is the acceptable standard? The preaching of the Word should take precedent. Every song that is sung should be one that could be sung before the throne of God for his glory, honor, and praise. That is the measure of worship, not the entertainment or emotional value. But, does it honor God?

The Water Spout of Worship

Everything in the early church pointed to the teaching and preaching of the apostles. The apostle Paul said,

> *Preach the word, be instant in season, out of season; reprove, rebuke, exhort with all long suffering and doctrine. For the time will come when*

they will not endure sound doctrine; but after their own lusts shall they heap to themselves teachers, having itching ears, and they shall turn away their ears from the truth, and shall be turned unto fables. (2 Timothy 4:2–4)

The word fables implies "myths, tales, and fiction." So in the last days, people will prefer stories, humor, and entertainment rather than Gospel preaching. Most churches are already there—they have fallen away from the truth.

Worship leaders prime the pump with prayer, Bible reading, and song so that the people can get to sound doctrine. The meaning behind the word doctrine is teaching. Evangelical churches are known to major on the proclamation of the Word of God. Romans 10:17 says, "So then faith cometh by hearing, and hearing by the word of God." It is the infallible, inerrant, and inspired book of the ages!

The pulpit is the "sacred desk." (Ezra preaching from a wood pulpit can be found in Nehemiah 8:4.) There have been great men of God through the ages that could preach straight from the heart. They believed in the total authority of the scriptures, and they gave their lives over to making it known to the people. That is why one of the sweetest names for a man of God is Preacher.

The man of God must be careful not to be in love with his own voice but to help the people hear the voice of God. He must preach the Word of God in context and be governed by applied truth. He must preach the whole counsel of God (Acts 20:27) and lead his people to fulfill the Great Commission of Jesus (Matthew 28:19–20).

The shepherd should preach expository messages much more than topical ones. An expositional message preaches verse by verse as it is given by the Holy Spirit. A topical message takes from here and there in the Bible to fit the message. Exposition builds the character of those who hear and heed the Word of the Lord. Topical messages can skim the surface and produce shallow belief.

Drinking Deep from the Truth

There are many ways to drink deep from the fountain of truth, which good Bible preaching and teaching produces: commemorating the ordinances and personally applying biblical truths during the invitation time. The altar call gives time and opportunity for the conviction of sin and the work of saving grace so that souls can be added to the church.

The church celebrates baptism and commemorates the Lord's Supper. Spiritually vital churches don't mind "getting wet"! They baptize new believers as a declaration of their faith and lifelong surrender to Jesus as their Lord and Savior. They see baptism as the first step of obedience, not necessary for salvation but as the fruit of salvation. Baptism tells the world that there is new life.

> *Buried with him in baptism, wherein also ye are risen with him though the faith of the operation of God, who hath raised him from the dead. (Collosians 2:12)*

When believers are baptized, they picture the death, burial, and resurrection of Jesus.

> *He that believeth and is baptized shall be saved. (Mark 16:16)*

Baptism does not save. Salvation is all of grace, but baptism tells what grace has done!

The Lord's Supper is commemorated too seldom by most evangelical churches. Though it is not counted as a sacrament ("means of grace"), it is an act of devotion and obedience. It is not the actual body and blood of Jesus but a symbol of his sacrifice for sinners. Bible churches should do it often and build the Gospel message around it.

The last moments of the service should be devoted to an invitation. People under conviction of sin may be invited to a counseling room. Some may want to bow and pray at the altar alone or with others. What is essential is to give people the opportunity to seek the Lord in reverence and surrender. Once the Spirit of God has had liberty to work, give a closing prayer and say the final blessing.

The Joy of Worship

Nothing should distract one in getting the people to God, his Word, and into his presence. That is the purpose of worship. The end of worship is total submission to Jesus as Lord and governor of the heart. It is a disservice to the people of God to allow a musician or any other personality to upstage the Word of the Lord and the glory due to him.

It is equally wrong to turn preaching into theatrics, comedy, and storytelling. A preacher's personality—or anyone else's for that matter—should not dominate the service—none but the person of Jesus, the only Savior who alone is worthy of worship. There is joy in worship—that is, if people can get to God. When worship leaders themselves fail to have an awareness of the presence of God, the people struggle too.

Worship should prepare the people in prayer that goes beyond the rooftop coupled with Bible reading that is able to pierce the indifferent heart. Songs should make the heart ready to receive the truth and obey any exhortation. When the Bible is opened, the people's hearts should be too so that they can receive it for thirty, sixty, and a hundredfold fruit. There should always be more honor for God's Word than a torrent of man's commentary.

True worship will permeate the church atmosphere with the presence of God so that people respond to Gospel appeals and calls for service. It will encourage the people of God to worship him and be devoted to him during the week so that Sundays are a celebration and culmination of worship all week! It will make people faithful to services because they will not want to miss them.

When such an experience of worship becomes the practice of the church, the people of God and the community will come to understand Hebrews 13:15: "By him therefore let us offer the sacrifice of praise to God continually, that is, the fruit of our lips giving thanks to his name." Souls will be saved, workers will be added, resources will flow, and nations will be transformed.

Summary Statements:

1. That is the measure of worship, not the entertainment or emotional value. But, does it honor God?
2. Exposition builds the character of those who hear and heed the Word of the Lord.
3. What is essential is to give people the opportunity to seek the Lord in reverence and surrender.
4. The end of worship is total submission to Jesus as Lord and governor of the heart.

What about storytelling? Didn't Jesus preach in parables?

Indeed, but there is a danger in replacing Bible teaching with stories and illustrations or delighting more in them than in the truths of scripture. Illustrations are great as long as they do not upstage the Word of God. There is an additional danger if the stories are more about a man than the Savior.

Notes

43

Can the people of God enjoy public worship if there has been no private worship during the week?

Yes, but it may take a bit more time to fire up the heart, unclog the ears, and open the eyes to spiritual truth. Worship can transform a heart at any time, but private worship makes public worship all the more meaningful. For a balanced spiritual life, both are necessary.

Who is the worship leader of the church service? Who orders the events and sets the timing for the service?

Some advocate the music minister or an associate who oversees the time of worship. Others see the lead pastor as in charge of every aspect of the service. It is challenging to prioritize and be timely if the lead pastor is not overseeing the service because he knows what must be done.

Chapter 8

Pure Evangelism

Christian leaders are reaping in church life the consequences of more than a century of "easy believism, "the salesmanship of the Gospel, and preaching God's love without his judgment. There are churches full of people with false conversions. Church members fall away from Christ because they have never been regenerated. Men have confused free grace with easy commitment.

Pure evangelism means counting the cost and hearing the clear Gospel call found in Matthew 16:24:

> *If any man will come after me,*
> *let him deny himself, and take*
> *up his cross, and follow me.*

Many separate the salvation experience from discipleship, but a closer examination of the New Testament does not validate the view that all true believers are not necessarily disciples:

> *And he that taketh not his*
> *cross, and followeth after me,*
> *is not worthy of me. (Matthew*
> *10:38)*

...Whosoever will come after me, let him deny himself, and take up his cross, and follow me. (Mark 8:34)

If any man come to me, and hate not his father, and mother, and wife, and children, and brethren, and sisters, yea, and his own life also, he cannot be my disciple. And whosoever doth not bear his cross, and come after me, cannot be my disciple. (Luke 14:26–27)

...Whosoever he be of you that forsaketh not all that he hath, he cannot be my disciple. (Luke 14:33)

Today's churches have a great divide between the salvation message and the discipleship imperative because there is the false belief in the church today that people can become Christians without changing a thing in their lifestyle. There is more concerned with church growth and numbers than with changed lives and real discipleship. That is why churches are in such a mess.

When there's inspirational services full of music and drama, people feel good, but they do not discern that the Spirit of God is grieved when the true meaning of the Gospel is missing and discipleship is void. That is not what Jesus died for. His message was not "Let's be friends, and "live however you want to." The apostle Paul said, "I am crucified with Christ..." (Galatians 2:20).

Pure evangelism is when people of faith proclaim the salvation message just as the Savior and the apostles had done. It requires repentance and breaking off sinful immorality and unrighteous living. There is a cross to carry, and that does not apply to physical ailments and the struggles common to all that live in this world. Carrying the cross means identifying totally with Christ by denying the sinful desires of the flesh. True salvation will bear the fruit of a righteous life.

Pictures of True Salvation

How about Zacchaeus?

Luke 19:1-10 tells the story of a notorious tax collector who got rich off his own people by defrauding them. When Jesus went to his house, he was never the same. He showed the fruits of repentance by giving away half his goods to the poor and repaying those he had cheated fourfold.

And Jesus said unto him, This day is salvation come to this house... (Luke 19:9)

Salvation today is just saying a prayer, getting wet, going to church for a little while, and then living like everyone else. Real transformation happens from the inside out.

Therefore if any man be in Christ, he is a new creature: old things are passed away; behold, all things are become new. (2 Corinthians 5:17)

When the Holy Spirit comes in, everything changes.

Saul of Tarsus was relentless in his hatred of Christians. There was no one who despised them more. He said, "...Beyond measure I persecuted the church of God, and wasted it..." (Galatians 1:13). The persecutor became the preacher so that the early church heard, "...he which persecuted us in times past now preacheth the faith which once he destroyed" (Galatians 1:23).

Christians know him by his new name: the apostle Paul. His salvation story is told three times in the Acts (9:1-19, 22:6-16, 26:12-18). He wrote thirteen of the New Testament epistles.

God forever changed Paul; he indeed was a new man.

> *And have put on the new man, which is renewed in knowledge after the image of him that created him...*
> *(Colossians 3:10)*

True salvation conforms believers to the image of Jesus (Romans 8:29) so that they join other believers in rising to "the stature and fullness of Christ" (Ephesians 4:13). If people in the church still act like the world, then they're not established in the Lord and are unsure of his saving grace. Peter said his people will "shew forth the praises of him who hath called you out of darkness into his marvelous light" (1 Peter 2:9).

The Necessity of the Cross

There is no Christian faith without the cross of Calvary. It is the place of atonement and is the sacrifice paid for sin. The hymn writers in times past understood the power of the cross. Here are the lines of blind composer Fanny Crosby, who wrote eight thousand hymns in her ninety-five years. This is "Near the Cross":

> Jesus, keep me near the cross
> There, a precious fountain
> Free to all, a healing stream
> Flows from Calvary's mountain
>
> Refrain:
> In the cross, in the cross
> Be my glory ever
> Till my ransomed soul shall find
> Rest beyond the river
>
> Near the cross, a trembling soul
> Love and mercy found me
> There, the Bright and Morning Star
> Sheds his beams around me [Refrain]

Notes

Near the cross! O Lamb of God
Bring its scenes before me
Help me walk from day to day
 With its shadow o'er me [Refrain]

Near the cross!
 I'll watch and wait
Hoping, trusting ever
Till I reach the golden strand
Just beyond the river [Refrain]

The apostle Paul was devoted to the cross. It was at the heart of the Gospel.

> *For the preaching of the cross is to them that perish foolishness; but unto us which are saved it is the power of God. (1 Corinthians 1:18)*

> *For I determined not to know any thing among you, save Jesus Christ, and him crucified. (1 Corinthians 2:2)*

> *But God forbid that I should glory, save in the cross of our Lord Jesus Christ, by whom the world is crucified unto me, and I unto the world. (Galatians 6:14)*

In Christian life, carrying the cross will mean self-denial, the rejection of self-will, and total surrender to do the will of God. When believers live the crucified life, they put to death the sinful desires of the flesh—like retribution, evil speaking, and sensuality. They will cast away spiritual laziness and serve the Lord in faithfulness and truth.

If men who serve the Lord are proud, power hungry, greedy, and have lustful, roving eyes, they have not been to the cross. They offer no contrast in their conduct to men of the world. If they feel like they have done enough in their service for the Lord, they have bypassed Calvary! The cross will make a man humble, pure, and true. Saving grace brings men and women to the foot of the cross, where personal sin is glaring and his pardon is secured.

Those who have been to the cross know how to love the Lord (who redeemed them), and know how to love their brothers and sisters, who share in the grace of God. When love for God is missing and enmity and hate rule the church, the love of Calvary is not real, regardless of the claim. Here is what the apostle of love wrote:

> *We love him, because he first loved us. If a man say, I love God, and hateth his brother, he is a liar: for he that loveth not his brother whom he hath seen, how can he love God whom he hath not seen? And this commandment have we from him, That he who loveth God love his brother also. (1 John 4:19–21)*

It is a rare church wherein love rules. Calvary is neglected when people are church members who do not love the Lord enough to worship and serve him, but can go all over creation to other places. When tempers flare and unkind words are spoken to someone's face—or, more often, behind their backs—people are not carrying their crosses. Their lack of love betrays them.

Remaining Fruit

When true salvation transforms a soul, they will bear fruit. A fruitless tree is cut down and cast into the fire. Moreover, a tree that bears corrupt fruit has the same destiny (Matthew 3:10, 7:16-20; John 15:6). Jesus said his disciples would bear fruit and when they did, it would be thirty, sixty, and a hundred fold (Matthew 13:8, 23).

> *Ye have not chosen me, but I have chosen you, and ordained you, that ye should go and bring forth fruit, and that your fruit should remain: that whatsoever ye shall ask of the Father in my name, he may give it you. (John 15:16)*

All true believers bear fruit. It is noteworthy that they go forth to bear it. They go into all the world—outside the bounds of Christian fellowship—to the lost and needy. Their work endures. They are a praying force that sees the Lord answering prayer as part of their fruit bearing.

How does that work in the life of the church? If someone comes into the fellowship with a profession of faith and obeys the Lord in baptism then serves for a season but is gone the next little while, they are not remaining fruit. What does 1 John 2:19 say?

> *They went out from us, but they were not of us; for if they had been of us, they would no doubt have continued with us: but they went out, that they might be made manifest that they were not all of us.*

Notes

49

The apostle minced no words, gave no excuses; he just said that they don't belong.

In the last days, the Bible says there will be a "waxing cold" (Matthew 24:12) and a great falling away (2 Thessalonians 2:3).

Many will say they know the Lord, but not do what he says (Matthew 7:21, Revelation 22:14). Churches and pulpits are full of such people. If church members live contrary to the Word of God, they produce either no fruit or bad fruit and will be cut off.

Peter called for abiding and abounding fruit in 2 Peter 1:5-9:

> *And beside this, giving all diligence, add to your faith virtue; and to your virtue knowledge; and to knowledge temperance; and to temperance patience; and to patience godliness; And to godliness brotherly kindness; and to brotherly kindness charity. For if these things be in you, and abound, they make you that ye shall neither be barren nor unfruitful in the knowledge of our Lord Jesus Christ. But he that lacketh these things is blind, and cannot see afar off, and hath forgotten that he was purged from his old sins.*

Second Peter 1:10-11 goes on with this exhortation:

> *Wherefore the rather, brethren, give diligence to make your calling and election sure: for if ye do these things, ye shall never fall; For so an entrance shall be ministered unto you abundantly into the everlasting kingdom of our Lord and Saviour Jesus Christ.*

When the Word of God goes in and the Holy Spirit reigns, fruit abounds in the believer's life. If not, then the heart is unplowed and in it sin prevails. This is not the abundance of material prosperity, but it is the bounty of spiritual fruitfulness. It is the Gospel ministry to hurting hearts and the building up of the true church.

Pure Evangelism Unifies the Church

There are church members who have to chew on something, take issue with a ministry or a minister, and voice their opposition to missions and evangelism. One pastor in Philadelphia, years ago, was fired because he was "too evangelistic." That is the sure sign of an unregenerate church. True churches unify around the command of Jesus to evangelize.

When lives are being transformed by saving grace, there is no greater joy or higher cause in the church. Everything else pales in comparison if Christians have God's heart for the world. As the church meets beneath the cross, knows the bite of sin, and experiences Christ's love, they will be humble enough to love the Lord and be faithful enough to cherish brothers and sisters who worship there too.

Paul wrote about unity in his epistle to Ephesus:

> *Endeavouring to keep the unity of the Spirit in the bond of peace. There is one body, and one Spirit, even as ye are called in one hope of your calling; One Lord, one faith, one baptism, One God and Father of all, who is above all, and through all, and in you all. (Ephesians 4:3-6)*

When the people of God have the Lord, they have unity in the Spirit. They have peace, which is a much-needed virtue in the church today. They share the same hope and calling. They lift up the Lord above all. Unity compels the church to serve, to seek out souls, and to encourage growth in the church.

It is crucial for the church to know what unity is not: it is not uniformity. Ecumenical is not a good term. Such movements in the church have a bent toward compromise, an acceptance of immorality, preferences for culture above biblical truth, and do not have a high view of scripture. Those kinds of churches comprise the false church in the last days.

Proper unity moves the church in one direction—from the place of worship to total surrender of the will to God-called service in evangelism, discipleship, and missions. Pure evangelism is counting the cost of following Jesus, repenting, learning love at the foot of Calvary, and bearing a bounty of fruit as disciples grow by grace through faith. Listen to the admonition of Colossians 2:6-7:

> *As ye have therefore received Christ Jesus the Lord, so walk ye in him: Rooted and built up in him, and stablished in the faith, as ye have been taught, abounding therein with thanksgiving.*

Notes

51

Summary Statements:

1. Real transformation happens from the inside out.
2. In Christian life, carrying the cross will mean self-denial, the rejection of self-will, and total surrender to do the will of God.
3. When the Word of God goes in and the Holy Spirit reigns, fruit abounds in the believer's life.
4. True churches unify around the command of Jesus to evangelize.

What is meant by "easy believism?"

It is the teaching that claims that if people believe in the right things, they are saved without having to make any lifestyle change. The devils in hell believed in all the right things, but they are still damned (James 2:19). People who have saving faith are saved from their sins. They become overcomers—they overcome sin that once defeated them—by the grace of God.

When Christians speak about going to the cross or carrying their cross, what are they saying?

It is a reference to self-denial according to Matthew 16:24. It is in direct contrast to those who believe in self-improvement, self-help, and self-reformation. Self is the problem. Self is bent toward sin and hell. Galatians 2:20 says that the life of the Christian is rightly defined as "not I, but Christ."

Chapter 9

Women in the Ministry

Everyone who is indwelt by the Holy Spirit has spiritual gifts and God-given ministry. Ladies of grace have a special calling. There were times in the history of the nation of Israel and in the early church when ladies took leadership roles, but they were out of the ordinary. There were no examples of women serving as pastors or deacons though Phebe has been cited in Romans 16:1.

The word translated there in some Bible versions as "deaconess" is better translated as "servant." It is never wise to base any principle on a single verse. All qualifications for pastors and deacons are for men as noted in 1 Timothy 3:1-13 and Titus 1:5-9. The church today has added women to the pulpit, pastoral ministries, and deacon service to accommodate the culture and times. The Lord intended pastors' and deacons' wives to serve beside them. If she is not qualified as 1 Timothy 3:11 says, then he is not qualified to serve: "Even so must their wives be grave, not slanderers, sober, faithful in all things." Both the deacon and his wife share in the calling. Many wives disqualify their husbands by their own conduct as a wife or a mother.

It is intriguing that in the context to qualify church leadership, these words are found just one chapter before:

In like manner also, that women adorn themselves in modest apparel, with shamefacedness and sobriety; not with braided hair, or gold, or pearls, or costly array; But (which becometh women professing godliness) with good works. Let the woman learn in silence with all subjection. But I suffer not a woman to teach, nor to usurp authority over the man, but to be in silence. For Adam was first formed, then Eve. And Adam was not deceived, but the woman being deceived was in the transgression. Notwithstanding she shall be saved in childbearing, if they continue in faith and charity and holiness with sobriety. (1 Timothy 2:9-15)

The answer to this difficult passage is not the suppression of women. Yet there is an admonition that runs contrary to popular church culture. Remember that the Lord lifted up women in his time and honored their service. Godly women are to be simple and modest. They're not to usurp the leadership of their father or husband. The word woman in reference to teaching is better translated as "wife" so she is not to continually lecture or teach her husband. As far as salvation by childbirth—that is to say that if she is married and becomes a mother—raising godly seed "saves" her from the shame of the curse.

A Biblical View of Women in Ministry

So, ladies can teach in the church. However, they should not have spiritual leadership or authority over men. They can team up with their husbands to teach in a couples' class. They can teach children and youth. The admonition is not to teach men as their superior. That is hard to swallow in today's culture, but it is God's created order. First Corinthians 11 reveals the truth. Church leaders must decide whether or not they will obey it.

But I would have you know, that the head of every man is Christ; and the head of the woman is the man; and the head of Christ is God. (1 Corinthians 11:3)

For the man is not of the woman: but the woman of the man. Neither was the man created for the woman; but the woman for the man. (1 Corinthians 11:8-9)

That is not a chauvinist's writing but the apostolic teaching inspired by the Spirit of God. No scripture is written for one era; it is timeless and applicable for those who want God's order rather than man's chaos as it is in the culture and in many churches today. It is amazing how many evangelicals say that they believe the Bible and yet make exceptions to such clear texts.

Women can be very sensitive and demanding in Christian fellowships. That is the very thing that the Spirit of God wanted to warn his people about. Here's an example of how women can be more comfortable with tradition and culture than with the revealed truth of scripture: All angels in the Bible are men. When that is taught, contrary to popular culture, women can become very upset and even angry! Even though it is true, that is beside the point.

Consider 1 Corinthians 11:5:

> But every woman that prayeth or prophesieth with her head uncovered dishonoureth her head: for that is even all one as if she were shaven.

This is proof that women did pray and prophesy in the early church, but they had their heads covered as a sign of submission. An uncovered head was like a shaven head, which was a sign of prostitution. Hair was the glory of the woman (1 Corinthians 11:15). Philip the evangelist's daughters were all prophets in the early church (Acts 21:8–9).

The biblical model for ladies in ministry is that they serve but not usurp. They are not to undermine the ministry of men of God. Women who do are not godly and obedient to scripture. In fact, they are worldly, and they hurt the witness of the church because they ignore the Word of God. When the role model for women in the Bible is compromised, the impact on the church is seismic.

The Errors of Suppression and Superiority

Often there are gaping holes in church leadership because of the vacancy of men and women stepping in to fill those roles. The result has been a feminization of the church that has driven many men away. It is evident in the sanctuary's appearance and décor, high church music, and silly dramas. Men can feel odd and out of place in such a setting.

The answer is not to suppress ladies, who often do much of the work of the ministry, nor is it to completely ice out strong male leaders for whom God intended the leadership of his church. The dominance of women in church leadership is contrary to scripture because it places them in superiority over men in spiritual leadership. Yet there is an indispensable role that ladies have that men cannot easily fill.

What does the scripture say? Today the church is not asking that question anymore. Instead, they are asking

Notes

"What do other churches do?" or "What's popular?" The trends in church leadership on display in these times would not have been accepted fifty years ago. Leaders have forsaken historic Christian faith for expediency and appeasement. The Lord is not pleased when his people forsake his Word. When spiritual eyes are opened, the people of God can see how family life has followed the curse revealed in Genesis 3:16:

> Unto the woman he said, I will greatly multiply thy sorrow and thy conception; in sorrow thou shalt bring forth children; and thy desire shall be to thy husband, and he shall rule over thee.

Eve sinned and sin has consequences: sorrow in childbirth and a desire to rule over her husband (though he was made to rule over her). That was just the beginning of the battle of the sexes. In this day, too many men neglect their families. They can be unfaithful to their wives and children, leaving women to fight for the life of their families. Women have been forced into giving leadership and fulfilling role models that God never intended. In such cases, women's respect for men is lost. They are not inclined to give up what they have fought so hard for. Family life can become a downward spiral. The solution is to return to biblical role models.

Keepers at Home

Here is what the scriptures say in Titus 2:3-5:

> The aged women likewise, that they be in behaviour as becometh holiness, not false accusers, not given to much wine, teachers of good things; That they may teach the young women to be sober, to love their husbands, to love their children, To be discreet, chaste, keepers at home, good, obedient to their own husbands, that the word of God be not blasphemed.

The question is when it comes to the design and place of men and women in the church, "do we teach the Word of God anymore?" Many will be angry about these principles in the Bible, but their contention is with the Lord. There are at least three truths from the text that demand our attention.

The phrase "keeper at home" would be revolutionary today since so few women do stay at home and make their husbands and children their top priority. Most women do more and look better for their bosses than they do for their husbands and families. That does not negate work outside the home; it just places the precedent on the home.

Then there's another line that is no longer applied in churches: "That they may teach the young women to be... obedient to their own husbands..." Any woman who refuses to do so should have no leadership role in the church and no voice because she is living like an unbeliever. The church has come to the place where people can "take it or leave it" when it comes to the practice of the Word.

The final phrase says, "that the Word of God be not blasphemed." That is exactly what is happening inside the church today. The Bible is being ignored and disregarded by the very ones who say they love and honor it. It is not the world that is blaspheming. It is the church that blasphemes (abuses) the Word of God. There is little place in too many hearts to do what God says.

A huge part of discipleship is the mentoring of younger women by the older. Titus sets God's standard for ladies' teaching ministry in the church and their expected example. That is the place young ladies should be going to for counsel— not doctors who prescribe medication for their mood swings. They should seek help from ladies of grace—who have fought the fight, raised godly families, and had enduring marriages.

Recovering the Ministry for Ladies of Grace

What is needful in the church and in the home is not a rivalry of the sexes and not ladies of grace enslaved, dishonored, and held by the chains of generational abuse and bondage. That is the devil's way to trample on the service and the gifts of single ladies, wives, mothers, and widows to the hurt of all. It is no less the devil's ploy to be subject to the demands and domination of women.

The church must return to the divine design and biblical roles of the Sovereign Lord for the family and the people of God. When the often-quoted verse in Galatians was put in the sacred text, it was not about women in leadership, but it was for the sweet equality of saving grace.

> *There is neither Jew nor Greek, there is neither bond nor free, there is neither male nor female: for ye are all one in Christ Jesus. (Gala- tians 3:28)*

Men and women are both guilty of misinterpreting the Bible, but this one is obvious. It is not at all a proof for women to be in church leadership.

It is refreshing to work with ladies who serve with all their hearts and yet have no bark or bite in their work for the church. They do not try to shanghai a service. They do not criticize the men of God. They refuse to be a gossip or busybody. Unfortunately, there are women on the other end of the spectrum that cause much trouble and heartache and think that they are godly while they

Notes

57

violate the clear instruction of scripture.

The people of God can only recover biblical ministry if they get their understanding from the New Testament. It is sinful to suppress the gifts of ladies of grace; but it is just as sinful to define their roles by the ways of the world, where women claw and scratch at others for equality and superiority. All things are not equal in leadership. They are in the work of saving grace.

There are some men who are not qualified to be pastors and deacons because of providential hindrance or character. Young men who are untested (novices) should not lead the church. Women are not scripturally qualified to serve as pastors and deacons though they may be almost indispensable as pastors' wives and deacons' wives. God will bless the church that honors the bounds he has set for leadership.

Regardless of what the Bible teaches, most people are going to revert to their feelings on such sensitive issues as women in ministry. "It just doesn't feel right," some will say. Truth runs up against our feelings a lot of the time.

The great-grandmother of the author and her sister started an Assembly of God church up on a mountain out in the Midwest. That is part of his heritage. We do not negate any gospel work when it is true, but we want our plumbline to be the Bible only.

Summary Statements:

1. The biblical model for ladies in ministry is that they serve but not usurp.
2. The dominance of women in church leadership is contrary to scripture because it places them in superiority over men in spiritual leadership.
3. The phrase "keeper at home" would be revolutionary today since so few women do stay at home and make their husbands and children their top priority.
4. The church must return to the divine design and biblical roles of the Sovereign Lord for the family and the people of God.

Why do people become so defensive about values that have no foundation in the Bible?

One example that was cited was the image of angels. In most cultures, they are depicted as women and children. That is true for most church dramas. The Bible shows angels to be men who are warriors and messengers. When cultural values are challenged, ungodly attitudes can arise.

Should women who refuse to practice a biblical role model have no leadership and voice in the church? Is that realistic?

Truthfully, most churches live a thousand miles from the pages of the scripture while they live right next door to the cultural demands for Christian ministry. The right biblical roles cannot be expected to be put in place until church leadership is reserved for those who believe in biblical authority and practice. It is realistic for the obedient church.

Don't some ladies need a doctor's care and medication to deal with the trauma and sorrows of life?

Indeed, doctors and medical counselors are needful; but when medications are given to alter the mind and mood rather than to give time to grieve and work through troubles of the soul through personal devotions and compassionate discipleship, then God is factored out and healing is postponed indefinitely.

Notes

59

Chapter 10

Biblical Leadership

How do dedicated Christians get leadership right in the church? Line up with the scriptures and get the church to match up with the practices of the New Testament. If the qualifications of primary leadership in the Bible is tracked for a period of at least fifteen generations (a generation can be up to one hundred years), it is the men of God who are selected to do the work of overseeing ministry.

Those men have moral and spiritual qualities that make them fit to lead. They are not perfect men; but they are not immoral, unethical, or given to error either. This is a matter of spiritual leadership, not civil authority. Paul wrote in 1 Timothy 3:4-5 about the man of God's family life:

> *One that ruleth well his own house, having his children in subjection with all gravity; (For if a man know not how to rule his own house, how shall he take care of the church of God?)*

Many will disagree, but the Bible teaches that if that is not the case, a man ought not to serve. This reference applies to pastoral leadership, but being an example in family life is true for deacon service as well.

That would take a lot of men who have unruly children, non-submissive wives, and unbelieving families out of pastoral ministry. A church has to decide if they are going to create their own standard or obey the Lord. Most churches readily compromise because they are not truthfully Word- based. Each church will either line up with the Word or with the world.

Biblical leadership is about character. It is a plurality of men who know the Word of God and are men of prayer. These men are leaders—not negotiators, not necessarily adept at church tug-of-wars. They are not politicians in a democracy. The church does not come together to vote but to minister. The clear instructions of the Word of God are not up for debate.

There is little evidence of ballots (casting lots) in the early assembly except for those used to replace Judas Iscariot in Acts 1. When we examine the Jerusalem Council in Acts 15, we find that it was the apostles who decided what to require of Gentile converts.

The pastors are not to be autocratic and dictators. They are to come together around New Testament principles and real prayer to discern the leadership of the Spirit of God. They are to be totally accountable to each other. Deacons are servants and, therefore, have no ruling authority. If a church has only one pastor, then other qualified spiritual leaders should be trained and ordained.

There is not a New Testament example of a church with just one pastor. When Titus was establishing churches in Crete, a hard and stony Gospel field, the apostle Paul instructed him in Titus 1:5:

> *For this cause left I thee in Crete, that thou shouldest set in order the things that are wanting, and ordain elders in every city, as I had appointed thee...*

Leadership is "wanting" in many churches today because there is one overworked pastor and a few deacons that are qualified only as servants. In this day and time, deacons are not usually men of the Word or of prayer, yet they view their leadership as equal to the pastors'. Typical in such churches, the pastors are short lived, and the deacons hire another pastor to do the work they are unwilling to do.

Pastors are Men of Character

Pastors, who practice godliness, are examples to the flock (1 Peter 5:3). Such men of God are to be blameless, the husband of one wife, vigilant, sober, well behaved, given to hospitality, ready to teach, not given to wine, not combative, not greedy, but patient, not proud, and well-thought-of in the community. Furthermore, they are to have faithful children, not self-willed and angry.

Qualified pastors are to be lovers of good men (no sexual reference here)—men who are just, holy, self-controlled, and able to teach sound doctrine and who hold fast to the Word. All of these traits are named in 1 Timothy 3:1-7 and in Titus 1:5-16. The greater portion

Notes

61

of the Titus passage speaks of the man of God's ability to deal with gainsayers, who plague many churches today. It is a shame that few men are able to stop them.

In Africa, South and Central America, and Asia, (just like in America) too many pastors have broken families. Those kinds of church leaders are not examples. In fact, they too often mimic their cultures. If men are prone to beating their wives, expect them to do most of the household work and provide for the family, wives may get identical treatment in pastors' homes!

Any man who beats his wife and does not provide for his own household has a hard time making the case as a believer, let alone as a man of God.

> *But if any provide not for his own, and specially for those of his own house,*
> *he hath denied the faith, and is worse than an infidel. (1 Timothy 5:8)*

A church deserves godly husbands and fathers as their shepherds. Otherwise, there are not men of character leading the church, which the Lord died to save. Wives become embittered, and children rebel against such hypocrisy. If the church compromises for one so-called man of God, they will compromise with others. Soon there will be no one fit to lead. Today, all too often the church is a mockery of unfit, ungodly, unscriptural, and unethical leadership.

Men of God Work with other Men of God

Leaders have a tendency for having a strong ego, and ministers are no exception. True men of God are tempered by the Word and prayer, and they learn hard lessons in humility. God-called men exalt the Lord and live for his glory. Men of God are spiritual warriors and warriors tend to love other warriors because they know what their own struggles are like. They know how it is to be on the frontlines of spiritual conflict. They know how it is to fight pride and selfishness.

There is a devilish development in parts of church life around the globe: single-pastor-led churches are dominated by one personality who does not share the pulpit, does not develop young pastor candidates, and discourages others from teaching the Word of God on their turf. It is understandable because other pastors can cause trouble, but it is still not right.

The Bible is relevant for today. Pastors are to "perfect" the saints for the work of ministry for the building up of the body of Christ (Ephesians 4:12). The more ministries that go on in the church and community, the more people are reached and encouraged in the faith. The Lord intended the church to be led by a plurality of humble men of God, not men with their own followings.

Even when a plurality of "qualified" men is in place and they serve the people well, there must be a point man or a chief elder and pastor. Like a husband-and-wife kinship, wherein they are co-regents in the home, only one has the spiritual authority and responsibility to make the final call for the home. The husband is wise to listen to his wife, but he is the leader and ultimately has the final say.

Pastors Make the Calls of Leadership

Churches can easily fall into the belief and practice that everyone has equal footing in decision-making. Knowing a little about the Bible, having many years of experience in church life, or giving great sums of money won't qualify people to give spiritual direction to the church. Preachers of the Gospel, who serve as pastors fully qualified and tempered by real Christian ministry, are the only ones that should give directions to the work of the church.

Spiritual men should lead the church, not untested and unproven believers. It is nonsensical to have people make leadership decisions when they have no charge or gifting from the Lord to do so. The people of God may indeed be spiritual and established in the knowledge and application of the scriptures, but if that is so, they would want God- appointed men to lead them.

Not all pastors are wise, humble, or even sincere, but they are the ones the Bible places at the helm of the ship. They are the ones that God has called to lead. The church is to obey their leaders and not hinder their own standing with the Lord. Hebrews 13 has the following two strong admonitions to that affect:

> *Remember them which have rule over you, who have spoken unto you the word of God: whose faith follow, considering the end of their conversation. (Heb.13:7)*

> *Obey them which have rule over you, and submit yourselves: for they watch for your souls, as they that must give account, that they may do it with joy, and not with grief: for that is unprofitable for you. (Heb. 13:17)*

Note that both passages say pastors "have the rule over you." That is God's order.

When the Bible says, "They that must give account," it not only speaks of accounting for the way pastors serve the people but also of accounting for the way the people serve the Lord. Pastors are the spiritual authorities over their people. They will report to the Lord about whether the people were righteous or not. The people of God need to take care in how they obey their pastors!

Notes

Men of God Represent the Chief Shepherd

Men of God are Satan's targets. It was true in Moses's day as the mixed multitude fought him and murmured again and again. The kings persecuted the prophets in the days of Israel and during Judah's decline. The religious elite of the first century, who were not true in doctrine or character, fought God in the flesh and the men Jesus chose. Every man of God is a target when he leads out.

The truth is that the people who are right with the Lord will honor men of God, and those who are not will fight them. It is not that only few in the world find the Lord. As a matter of fact, few in the church actually do! Satan works inside the church all the more because he does not want saving grace to be the banner of the church or the Great Commission to be its heartbeat. The devil likes everything but doing the work of evangelism, discipleship, and missions.

God calls men from their mother's womb to be his servants (Jer. 1:5). Add Moses, John the Baptist, and Paul the Apostle to a long list of men for whom God called to his service.

> Paul, an apostle, (not of men, neither by man, but by Jesus Christ, and God the Father, who raised him from the dead)... (Galatians 1:1).

These men were men of God, not men of men.

That is the trouble in the church today: they are hiring men of men. Another word for it would be politicians. Men of God do the bidding of their Master, obey the scriptures, order the church as it is written in the scriptures, and remain totally committed to Gospel work. They are kingdom builders—not in their own names but in the name of the Lord Jesus, the chief Shepherd.

These men of God have moral and spiritual character that serves the church by example in family life and personal devotion, in public witness and missionary fervor. They are the kind of men that will love and work with other godly men who share the same passion for Jesus and his truth. They lay aside their pride and take up his humble service.

They make the calls in the life of the church. They are leaders, so they govern the church as God has appointed them to do. To divest people of their vote and voice is not acceptable to most. There is a reason congregational churches split and divide so much. It is always a poor testimony to the community.

Elder-led churches can also have their divisions, but that is due to putting unspiritual men in place. Men filled with the Spirit will find God's pleasure as they search the scriptures and pray together. The church is all about doing the will of God and obeying the Word of God. The best candidates for governing the church are the men God has called and placed there.

The question is will Bible believers argue with the Bible? Will they violate God's design for the church?

If churches choose tradition and culture above the truth, then they open the door to the world and the devil. If the people of God follow the blueprint of the New Testament, the church will be centered on ministry and not debate. The people will come together for worship and not fall prey to shallow personalities enamored with self.

Summary Statements:

1. A church deserves godly husbands and fathers as their shepherds.
2. The Lord intended the church to be led by a plurality of humble men of God.
3. Spiritual men should lead the church, not untested and unproven believers.
4. The truth is the people who are right with the Lord will honor men of God, and those who are not will fight them.

Why are single pastor led churches so contrary to the New Testament?

There are no examples in the Bible for that kind of leadership—none. All men are fallible and, at times, lack discretion, so there needs to be accountability among pastor brothers. Men of God are also gifted differently, and when more than one man leads the church, the gifts can complement each other for greater service to the people of God. Plurality of leadership is God's design for his church.

What are the spiritual responsibilities of biblical leaders?

They are to preach the Word of God and apply it. They are called to intercede for their people. Then men of God are to equip the saints to do the work of ministry.

Many evangelical churches are based on congregational government and expect to vote and voice their opinions over church action. How do you return to the biblical model of leadership without upsetting the church?

Here are a few practical ways it can be done.

Every church setting is different. Returning to the practice of scripture does not happen in most churches without a close examination of God's design for the church and a lot of patience on the part of leaders to move the people from the church culture to the New Testament standards.

Notes

1. Godly men serve as the shepherds of the church with a point man who leads the others by consent and in full agreement (if at all possible).
2. These men are to be proven in character—with knowledge and application of the scripture (especially New Testament practices)—and be men of prayer.
3. They have a heart for the people as true shepherds to listen to them, speak the truth, care for their souls, and lead them to trust and obey.
4. These men of God have godly wives who are not gossips, busybodies, and slanderers. These ladies of grace know the Word and prayer.
5. The biblical model brings the church together so that the members can be equipped to minister and fulfill the Great Commission of Jesus—not to vote.
6. For the cause of peace, if there needs to be a format for the people to have a voice in decision-making, it is wise to call for affirmation and not a vote.
7. If the shepherds are properly caring for the flock, they will listen to the cries of the sheep. Yet shepherds have gifts of leadership that the sheep lack.
8. Such times of affirmation may be set for confirming matters of electing leadership, approving budgets, purchasing property, and doing construction.
9. In such a way, the church can come together not for controversy, strong opinions, and division but for ministry, learning, and times of true worship.
10. This would prevent the church from giving sway to fighting and discord, which would mar their witness and make void any atmosphere of worship.
11. Congregational governed churches have a history of division and strife. Though they often have a true message, it can be invalidated by fighting.
12. Congregational churches are also noted for their people going from church to church due to offenses which further hurt the cause of the Gospel.

If the people of God will follow the New Testament principles for the church, then strife, division, and conflict would be tamed by men who are governed by the Word of God and prayer. Scorners would lose their place in the church.

Chapter 11

Revival and Awakening

Viewpoints on revival and awakening are varied: Some see it as a series of meetings led by a guest preacher. Others see revival as needed, but do not believe it is connected to special services. Instead, it is getting the church to apply the truth of the Word of God every day as a lifestyle— that obedience to the Gospel message brings about revival in the church and awakening in the land. Still others see revival and awakening as an emotional wave that rises and falls on the whims of fickle men.

A great number of Bible-based churches have held revival events once or twice a year for decades and have only had a few lasting fruits. There has been overall disappointment because the emotional surges revivals can bring soon return to a low tide in church morale. Guest preachers can be manipulative against a pastor's expressed wishes, and too often, they are spiritually undiscerning.

When revival comes to the people of God, this is what happens: people rally around the Word, sinners find grace, hearts are transformed, and many are forever changed. The event can be worthwhile, but it is much better to be in continual revival with a high view of scripture where people are obedient to the preached text all the time.

There are many verses that speak to the revival of a nation or church. Some verses that may not have originally been intended for revival have been used that way, like Isaiah 41:18, which says,

> *I will open rivers in high places, and fountains in the midst of the valleys: I will make the wilderness a pool of water, and the dry land springs of water.*

Then there are texts that do apply, like Psalm 85:6:

> *Wilt thou not revive us again: that thy people may rejoice in thee?*

And how about Acts 3:19?

> *Repent ye therefore, and be converted, that your sins may be blotted out, when the times of refreshing shall come from the presence of the Lord.*

There is little question that the church needs revival and communities need awakening. The distinction between the two is that revival brings life back to the church and awakening impacts the community with the manifested presence of God. The most effective and biblical way to experience revival is to exalt the Word and watch what happens when people put it to practice.

Revivals and Awakenings Happened in the Bible

Revival of errant Israel is seen in the book of Judges when God sent a lady (Deborah) or a man to call the nation back to the law. Renewal and restoration for the nations of Judah and Israel are also witnessed under righteous kings of Judah and dynamic prophets of Israel. Israel never had a righteous king. All the kings of Israel, without exception, were idolaters and worshippers of Baal.

Spiritual revival came in the days of Asa, Jehoshaphat, Hezekiah, and Josiah while spiritual awakening came during the time of Elijah, Elisha, and Jonah as they faithfully proclaimed the Word of the Lord to apostate Israel. Revival literally means "to make alive again." God calls his people back through righteous leadership.

Men of God call people back to compliance to the Word of God. The people who neglect the law of God abuse the grace of God. The nation that ignores the Word of God does so to their detriment and demise. The only hope for any nation is that the people of God be found faithful in prayer and fully committed to make known the glory of God. In short, the hope of a nation is God—and he is known through his people.

Romans 12:11 has a formula for personal revival: "Not slothful in business; fervent in spirit; serving the Lord..." Christians must be about the Master's business, keeping their spirits at a "boiling point," and ever willingly to serve the Lord. The loss of passion for the Lord is the result of spiritual laziness, a cold heart, and serving self. Revival brings people back to God and to the scriptures.

> *Nevertheless I have somewhat against thee, because thou hast left thy first love. Remember therefore from whence thou art fallen, and repent,*

and do the first works; or else I will come unto thee quickly, and will remove thy candlestick out of his place, except thou repent. (Revelation 2:4-5)

Revival alone can restore what has been lost. The revived spirit returns to the first love—Jesus. Revival is missing when his name is no longer as sweet on our lips as it once was. When salvation does not bring the joy it once did, the people of God are fallen and need to stand in love and true devotion once again.

It means the people of God are down and out. The Lord calls the church back to the first works of evangelism, discipleship, and missions. If they will not return, they can lose their light forever. They will go from being a church to being a club.

There have been Historic Revivals and Awakenings

Men like Girolamo Savonarola in 1482 brought awakening to Florence, Italy, where he served as a preacher and parish pastor. He was fearless, and the city flourished under his leadership as he called the church to repentance and faith. But in time, the powers of the city turned against him, and he was martyred. Revivalists deal with sin, and so it does not make them populists.

Jonathan Edwards may have been the greatest theologian on the American continent. He was a New England pastor in the 1740s when the First Great Awakening came. He had accepted the call to serve his grandfather's church, where God poured out his Spirit not only upon the church but upon the entire region. Yet in time that same church dismissed him as their pastor.

There have been movements of God in Wales, China, East Africa, Indonesia, and India in the previous century, when missionaries operated at a high level of spiritual life and churches multiplied as the population felt the effects as they lived out their faith. Revival of the church can result in the awakening of a continent. Testimonies and the mighty deeds of God sweep nations with new life.

Notes

Then again, there are some movements that go against the scripture and dishonor the Holy Spirit as aberrant, erroneous, and hyped-up, like the so-called Toronto Blessing in 1994 and the Brownsville "Revival" in 1995. Roaring, barking, and laughing characterized these meetings. These kinds of experiences are actually exaggerated and spurious and therefore do not bring glory to God.

What about Contemporary Revival Claims?

Besides false phenomena already named, there were unrighteous fruits that came out of the 1990s events. For example, the Apologetics Index [1] and the World Religions and Spirituality Project [2] revealed misrepresentation of the credentials of leaders—ten million dollars of debt incurred and unsubstantiated healings.

True revival is never built on lies, deception, and financial mismanagement. Awakening makes a community better, not worse. The work of the Holy Spirit exalts Christ, not men. It does not make a mockery of the Lord and his church. Revival and awakening make the Lord look good and bring glory to his name.

If manipulation and theatrics are the stuff of today's revivals, they are not in biblical proportions. They are the devil's imitations. Real revival takes us back to the Bible, not a far cry from it. The church that is experiencing refreshing from the presence of the Lord will not grieve the Holy Spirit of God. A revived spirit can clearly distinguish between what is false and what is true.

If the servants of the Lord, who know his Word and live by prayer, get sick at heart from what they witness, then what they are witnessing is not of God. We have much happening in the name of the Lord that have replaced the cross and real discipleship with godless gyrations and false teachers who teach all about health, wealth, and prosperity. These characters do not know Christ. They live for themselves and their own glory.

Second Timothy 3:1–5 forewarns of such pretenders who revive Satan's work in the littered landscape of error and immorality that only the biblically illiterate would call the church:

> *This know also, that in the last days perilous times shall come. For men shall be lovers of their own selves, covetous, boasters, proud, blasphemers, disobedient to parents, unthankful, unholy, Without natural affection, trucebreakers, false accusers, incontinent [without self-control], fierce, despisers of those that are good, Traitors, heady, high-minded, lovers of pleasures more than lovers of God; Having a form of godliness, but denying the power thereof: from such turn away.*

Genuine believers can be sure that if people are covetous, blasphemous, and high-minded, they are not revivalists but sin's purveyors. They know that revival upholds the attributes of God. Revival and awakening is always Bible centered and prayer driven.

How do we discern between the false and the true in this day? The same way that the apostles did! They spent time in the presence of the Lord while they applied the truth of the law and the

---

1   Jeffrey M. Spencer, "An Examination and Evaluation of the Brownsville Revival," in the Christian Apologetics Journal 2, no. 1, (Spring 1999). www.apologeticsindex.org/b79.html

2 . David G. Bromley and Amanda Tellefsen, "Brownsville Revival," (December 2011). www.wrs.vcu.edu/profiles/BrownsvilleRevival.htm

prophets that they had. Believers today must keep their Bibles open and be ready to obey what they read. Christians increase their discretion by praying and pouring out their hearts before God. Between the truth of the Word and the power of prayer, they know who is serving God.

> *Beloved, believe not every spirit, but try the spirits whether they are of God: because many false prophets are gone out into the world. (1 John 4:1)*

If so-called spiritual leaders have been immoral, unscriptural, and unethical in their dealings, they cannot lead the church back to God and revive hearts. They are not credible spiritual leaders and therefore should step down.

In these days, there are those who call themselves by the name of the Lord and seek to lead the church while they repeatedly file for divorce, cavort with male and/or female prostitutes, extort money, and boast of mighty works. Such leaders tell us why we are so desperate for true revival and awakening.

What happened to holiness and righteousness? That is the stuff of revival!

False teachers who dominate pretentious Christian networks (like *Trinity Broadcasting Network*) do ministry for a profit and cloak their lust and greed. They repulse the world and all true believers. Still, so many are deceived when they do not know the Bible!

What can be done to have heaven-sent revival? Know that real men of God are humble and not flashy. They live under the judgment of God. They know God is a consuming fire (Hebrew 12:29). Men of God understand that the Word of God is far superior to any of man's revelations as it has been tested by time. Revival brings people down on their knees and back to the Bible alone.

We have also a more sure word of prophecy; whereunto ye do well that ye take heed, as unto a light that shineth in a dark place, until the day dawns, and the

Notes

day star arise in your hearts: Knowing this first, that no prophecy of the scripture is of any private interpretation. For the prophecy came not in old time by the will of man: but holy men of God spake as they were moved by the Holy Ghost. (2 Peter 1:19–21)

Summary Statements:

1. Men of God call people back to the Word of God.
2. Revivalists deal with sin, and so it does not make them populists.
3. A revived spirit can clearly distinguish between what is false and true.
4. Men of God understand that the Word of God is far superior to any of man's revelations.

Does revival come by man meeting the conditions of God, or does it come from the sovereign act of God?

It comes from both. It is always sent by God— but man can prepare his heart by surrendering to the promptings of the Spirit, doing the will of God, and building the witness and light of the church.

What must happen for revival to come to the church?

It starts with personal revival in men's and women's hearts. The effects of sin will so grip a church that the people turn back to the Living God and break off their sins. The people of God then sow seeds of righteousness for a righteous harvest.

Do revival meetings help or hinder the church? Do revival meetings produce lasting results?

If they are God-dependent and God honoring, they help. They produce lasting fruits whether they are evident or not. If they are man-dependent and exalt the flesh, then those efforts amount to nothing.

Chapter 12

Church Planting

The highest form of all church activities after the spiritual essentials of applying biblical truth and heartfelt prayer is missions, and the highest level of missions is church planting. That is reproduction at its finest! It is the best way to make disciples and preserve a witness in a community. Church planting keeps on magnifying Christ long after mission teams go back home—that is, if the church matches the biblical pattern and not the cultural models.

God blesses what he designs. If church planting means having slick advertisements, an electric keyboard, and a church bus, then somehow we missed the point. All those things have nothing to do with biblical faith. Church planting must be bigger than buildings—so big that it transforms communities.

Many churches have bought property and built facilities but have yet to touch the hearts of those in their communities. Many perish within sight of the cross set on a church house but have never seen people deny themselves fully enough to love those who are lost in Jesus's name. The true church moves beyond activities to a Christian lifestyle of evangelism, discipleship, and missions, which are best seen in the development of new churches.

Churches can be planted in schools, the marketplace, homes, and even under a tree. Like any New Testament model, what is required is godly leadership, sacrificial giving, bold witnessing, and a love for people. New churches have a greater capacity to reach all kinds of people, to build up family life, and to minister to youth without pointless programs.

The commitment to multiply churches should be in the "DNA" of every church, but most traditional congregations are not going to the harvest fields to build the kingdom. The more a church gives out, the more they will grow and be blessed by the Lord. When people love missions and multiply churches through both the hard and the sweet times, God will make his glory known there.

Church Planting is the Model of the Churches of the Acts

Congregations multiply because that is the fruit of the Word of God—whether it is in times of peace or persecution. The distinction of the church in Acts was wholehearted devotion. They did not have faith in half measures.

Read the record of the Acts of the Holy Spirit:

> And believers were the more added to the Lord, multitudes both of men and women. (Acts 5:14)

> And daily in the temple, and in every house, they ceased not to teach and preach Jesus Christ. (Acts 5:42)

> And the Word of God increased; and the number of the disciples multiplied in Jerusalem greatly; and a great company of the priests were obedient to the faith. (Acts 6:7)

> Then had the churches rest throughout all Judaea and Galilee and Samaria, and were edified; and walking in the fear of the Lord, and in the comfort of the Holy Ghost, were multiplied. (Acts 9:31)

> But the word of God grew and multiplied. (Acts 12:24)

> And the word of the Lord was published throughout all the region. (Acts 13:49)

> And so were the churches established in the faith, and increased in number daily. (Acts 16:5)

> So mightily grew the word of God and prevailed. (Acts 19:20)

There is a direct relationship between the Word of God, wholehearted faith, and the growth of the church (in terms of adding disciples and multiplying churches). As the Word of the Lord was magnified, the Lord added and multiplied. The church of the Acts worked on the heart, transformed the mind, and grew the soul.

The church is never more in trouble than when there is not growth and reproduction. An inwardly focused church is sin sick while an outward focused ministry is vibrant and healthy. The book of Acts reveals a different breed of believers who responded to persecution with grace and boldness and kept fulfilling the exhortation in Acts 1:8:

> *But ye shall receive power, after that the Holy Ghost is come upon you: and ye shall be witnesses unto me both in Jerusalem, and in all Judaea, and in Samaria, and unto the uttermost part of the earth.*

Amazingly, the early church took to heart what the Master said: they witnessed to the saving grace and the mighty Word of God. The fruits were not just new believers but new churches too. Whenever leaders fail to see new life in the church and new churches in the kingdom, they operate in the flesh and not by the power of the Holy Ghost.

The Labor Pains and Birth of a Church

Satan is going to fight the starting of new churches. He will oppose the very idea of investing in new churches through church leaders who want to continue committing 90 percent of the budget to inside the church. Most will say, "Charity starts at home" or "There are plenty of needs right here." But if people read their Bibles closely, they will discover that the church described in the book of Acts gave 90 percent outside the church.

Birthing a church is a painful process, not only because of so-called "Christian" opposition inside church leadership but also because of other churches that may feel threatened. The majority of the populace in most regions of the world is not faithful to a church, so the un-churched need to be brought to a place of worship and service. New churches reach the lost more effectively.

Then there are the obstacles of finding a sponsoring

church and supporters, identifying a meeting place, calling together a leadership team, and securing the finances. New churches are much more warmhearted and open than established churches with regard to reaching out to all kinds of people—they reach out to those that a conventional church cannot or simply don't.

There are birth pains that are particular to every work and every location, but it is worth each point of agony when people begin to come to transforming grace and find mercy in the Lord. When those who have never bent their knees or sung "Jesus is Lord" join in the heavenly chorus, it is worth it all! It is like the joy of parents when they finally get to hold their baby after a long labor.

New churches are more apt to start more churches. They realize that there is spiritual blessing in doing church God's way. When a church gives away workers, what were once called "seed families" to start a new church, God often replaces those who go out with even more workers. Faithful people love a working church that keep giving themselves away to kingdom service.

Sweet Multiplication

The big story behind the church of Acts is multiplication. The more hearts that are fully devoted to Jesus, the greater the impact in a church and community. Today, most churches are doing well to survive and to break even, but that is ministry without the blessing of the Holy Spirit. When he is present, his bounty is evident. A fruitful church makes the critics ashamed.

If Christian ministries want to multiply believers and churches, they must first multiply leaders. Along with making disciples, a church that is serious about extending their witness to other communities must also develop leaders. Churches must have a climate for calling out leaders and encouraging leadership training, wherein the pastors have freedom to direct the work of ministry so that others are encouraged to work in leadership roles. If leadership is nothing but protracted contention with a lot of bureaucracy, then the list of new recruits will be short. An environment wherein leaders are loved and respected encourages others to want to train and to serve. The essential element of leadership is that those who lead are examples and practical in their faith. They should be the first to witness and enlist in mission outreaches.

If you want sweet multiplication, it should start with leadership. Good leadership makes for practical discipleship and church reproduction. If churches miss it in leadership, the whole organization is weak. Every officer of the church should be totally committed to sharing the faith, doing mission work, and making disciples. If not, they should not be leaders!

If Churches Do Not Add and Multiply, They Subtract and Divide

Consider what happens in most churches: they do not have a godly core committed to evangelism, discipleship, and missions. Their churches do everything but what the church of the Acts did. As a result, they subtract and divide rather than add and multiply. Where there are deductions and divisions in a church, you can be sure that the truly godly are not the movers and shakers.

Men of God must recall the words of Exodus 32:26:

Then Moses stood in the gate of the camp, and said, Who is on the Lord's side? let him come unto me. And all the sons of Levi gathered themselves together unto him.

Every church must decide whether they will do the Lord's work or man's. Most church leaders are doing the work of man. That is why the math is going the wrong way and the church is losing ground to the enemy. As it was in Moses's day, the crux of the matter is idolatry—serving lesser gods, not the Lord God.

The incident in Exodus is at the foot of Mount Sinai, where Aaron had fashioned a golden calf. In the church today, there are many golden calves: stage productions, feel- good speaking, gathering knowledge without action, giving tokens to missions but never actually doing missions, and going to meetings that are more focused on business than on prayer. It is the picture of a carnal church.

Carnal churches do not grow spiritually and prepare people for the day of the Lord. They give folks religion to soothe their guilty consciences and play the game they call church. Spirit-filled churches cannot help but grow—spiritually and numerically. Their growth is hard to track because they keep sending their people out to start new ministries and new churches. They *build* the kingdom.

Most nominal Christians do not want any pain or suffering in their tidbit of service for the Lord. They do not believe that the church is worth the aggravation that comes with working with less-than-perfect people. If people opt out of pain in life, they also miss out on love, birthing babies, and raising teenagers! Today the church loves to laugh but does not want to weep and wrestle over souls.

If the church is not enjoying sweet multiplication, it may be that they have forsaken godly standards and have stopped winning souls, making disciples, and doing mission work. All of these activities of the church in the Acts caused the Word of God to be magnified and believers to be multiplied. Programs, pageantry, and public opinion polls will not return the church back to the greatness of honoring God.

Notes

77

Summary Statements:

1. Whenever leaders fail to see new life in the church and new churches in the kingdom, they operate in the flesh and not by the power of the Holy Ghost.
2. Faithful people love a working church that keep giving themselves away to kingdom service.
3. Every officer of the church should be totally committed to sharing the faith, going on missions, and making disciples.
4. If the church is not enjoying sweet multiplication, it may be that they have forsaken godly standards and have stopped winning souls, making disciples, and doing mission work.

Don't we have enough churches?

No, we don't. Never. Not until all people on the face of the earth know the Lord Jesus, are discipled, and give their hearts to kingdom service. Churches die, and many are barely in existence because members fall away from ministries that are impractical and lifeless. New churches reach more people and actually take measures to reach the unreached.

What are the advantages of starting churches compared to working with an established church?

New churches do not have a history of broken relationships and a poor testimony. Not every church has been guilty of ungodly actions, but healthy churches reproduce and find ways to reach out to those who are not engaged in the faith with the truth of the Gospel. New churches have less bureaucracy, have open leadership, and are much more proactive.

What essential elements make a church a church?

It is not the building as much as it is biblical leadership, faithfulness to make disciples, meeting in a place for prayer and worship where baptism and the Lord's Supper are practiced and where the people are equipped to do the work of ministry. The church is a people of Christian faith who are "called out" from the world to meet around the Word of God and the Great Commission of Jesus.

Part II

Ladies of Grace Devotionals

Chapter 1

Woman's God-Given Design

*And the Lord God said, It is not good that the man should be alone; I will
make him an help meet for him. —Genesis 2:18-25*

There is nothing more fulfilling than to function according to our God-given design. It is tragic that women have chosen to cultivate a cultural mind-set. They have adopted the values and philosophies of the world around them rather than choosing to think biblically. This mind-set has distorted their view of men and how they themselves function in the home as wife and mother.

What confusion our enemy, the god of this world, has caused with rapid destruction!

God made man and woman "co-stewards" of creation, but he certainly gave them very different roles. They are God-given and divinely assigned. Woman was to be a helpmeet (helper). This means that a woman complements and completes. You see, man is incomplete without woman and she fulfills his need for a companion. God also created the woman to be a "life giver"—the vessel by which children would be born and nurtured. What a beautiful responsibility—one that requires extreme sacrifice and immense love.

But first, women, must learn to embrace God's divine order given in 1 Corinthians 11:3:

> *But I would have you know, that the head of every man is Christ; and the
> head of the woman is man; and the head of Christ is God.*

God, Christ, man, and then woman. In that order, women are given a unique function. When we long to know truth, walk in it and honor God, we inherit a wellspring of blessing. But more importantly, we are a sweet aroma to our Heavenly Father.

Culture teaches the woman to be independent in spirit. Satan has convinced her that her roles as wife, mother, and keeper of the home are not satisfying enough. Believers, however, understand that true satisfaction will be met in obedience to Christ and his Word alone!

Chapter 2

A Woman's Greatest Temptation

Unto the woman he said, I will greatly multiply thy sorrow and thy conception; in sorrow thou shalt bring forth children; and thy desire shall be to thy husband, and he shall rule over thee. —Genesis 3:16

Every woman falls under the curse of Genesis 3:16. Not only will she experience pain in childbirth while on this earth, but this scripture also tells us that her "desire" shall be for her husband. This does not mean sexual desire but the desire to "lord over" him. But by God's divine design, the husband shall rule over her.

What is her temptation? In that word desire, we find her struggle. Her flesh wants to "rule over," to take control of, to undermine his authority, and to act independently from her husband (just as Eve did). That sums it up!

Our only hope is in Christ Jesus in whom we are overcomers. We must continually walk by the Spirit, refuse to feed the flesh, all the while striving to lovingly and willingly submit to our spouse. May we always yield to the Word of truth with hearts of clay and humility!

Notes

Questions to Ask Yourself:

1. Does my husband know that I am fully committed to loving, helping, and serving him with a kind and gentle servant's spirit?
2. Do I bless him and pray for him as I should?
3. Am I responding to his leadership lovingly?
4. Am I contentious and always having the need to speak the last word?
5. When he disciplines the children, do I jump to their defense, usurping his authority?
6. Do I consult with my spouse concerning important matters?

Chapter 3

Becoming a Woman of Great Influence

Who can find a virtuous woman? for her price is far above rubies. —Proverbs 31:10

The woman in Proverbs 31 is one of great influence—so much so that her husband is known in the city gates and her children all call her blessed. In the Hebrew language the word for virtuous is hayil. It means "strength, wealth, and army",[1] carrying the idea of force and influence. Well, I like to say that the Proverbs 31 woman has the strength, might, and influence of an army! She does all things with extreme excellence. Her success does not depend on her physical beauty, but it is due to her spiritual life.

If we look at the words *far above*, we find that in Hebrew it means "remote" and "distant."[2] Therefore, she does exist but is very hard to find (rare indeed!)

Verse 30 reminds us that she "feareth the Lord." John MacArthur, author of The MacArthur Study Bible, says, "The fear of the Lord is a state of mind in which one's own attitudes, will, feelings, deeds, and goals are exchanged for God's." The fear of God is the beginning of knowledge

---

1 Warren Baker and Eugene Carpenter, The Complete Word Study Dictionary-Old Testament, AMG Publishers, Chattanooga (October 2003), p. 334.
2 Ibid, p.1047

Notes

and wisdom. Herein lies her great success! Her life shows the fruits of her devotion to him alone.

So, ladies, may our "influence" at home, at work, in the harvest fields, and in church be fueled by our deep reverence (fear) of God!

Chapter 4

Recognizing Your Enemy

Above all, taking the shield of faith, wherewith ye shall be able to quench all the fiery darts of the wicked.
—Ephesians 6:16

Since the beginning, when the serpent entered the picture in Genesis, war was declared! First Peter 5:8 tells us that the devil is a roaring lion that's "seeking whom he may devour." After being in the ministry for thirty plus years, I am convinced that those in leadership positions become "targets" for the wicked one. A pastor, his wife, and his children are marked!

A wife of a ministry leader needs to recognize the enemy and his tactics. Her prayers on behalf of her husband and children are crucial, and her faith is the key.

The following are some important points to remember:

1. Satan is your accuser (Revelation 12:10–11). He charges you with an offense! He claims you have done wrong with the ultimate hope that God will forsake you.
2. Satan has a host of helpers (Ephesians 6:11–12). We see principalities, powers, and rulers of darkness.

Notes

Verse 11 reminds us with the word wiles that he has devised carefully laid-out schemes. This word involves deception and extreme cleverness. He strikes with precision!

3. Faith is our victory (1 John 5:4-5). We are, indeed, overcomers, and God has blessed us with a piece of armor—the shield of faith—that is able to put out any fiery darts of temptation thrown at us. After all, "If God be for us, who can be against us?" (Romans 8:31)

4. The devil is a liar (John 8:44). There is no truth in him! How often do you find yourself listening to his lies?

5. Satan is an opportunist (1 Peter 5:8). He looks for an avenue to bring destruction upon you, your husband and your children.

Ladies, we are to be diligent and steadfast concerning the practice of prayer: the greatest position you and I can be in to fight the wicked one is *on our knees*. May we be found faithful!

Chapter 5

Entering In

But thou, when thou prayest, enter into thy closet, and when thou hast shut thy door, pray to thy Father which is in secret; and thy Father which seeth in secret shall reward thee openly. —Matthew 6:6

This verse Matthew 6:6 fits into a series of teachings in which Christ wanted to make sure that the disciples did not imitate the hypocrites. He was exposing the self-righteousness of the Pharisees (they thrived on gaining the admiration of others). And yet there are other important truths for you and me to glean too.

Entering into our closet is an act of pure worship. It requires maximum effort and diligence of those practices we oftentimes fear: discipline, self-examination, repentance, brokenness, humility, dying to self, keeping quiet, listening, and waiting upon our Father. No wonder we are not "entering in!"

The word *closet* means "secret room" or "storehouse." In the biblical days, it was a private or inner room—a secret place where people hid their treasures and most-valued pieces. Think about your closet: just you and God alone. Quiet. His presence. There is awe, a

Notes

silence, a bowing down of oneself in worship.

Think of the treasures that await you in this hidden place: fellowship and intimacy with the Father, the remembrance of his promises rising up to strengthen your heart, the Spirit's comfort and conviction bringing brokenness, our inheritance of peace, forgiveness, restored hope, refreshment and yes, radical change!

What excuses justify your neglect?

No matter what excuses you may have, we are still given the command to "enter in."

Why do we neglect? Why do we continue on with our own agenda? Why, oh why, do we miss out when the promise in Matthew 6:6 is so incredible?

The one who sees you in secret will reward you out in the open! He will literally "cause to shine" the very answers to your prayers.

But you have to remember that you must ask in faith!

Chapter 6

Shut Thy Door

*...And when thou hast shut
thy door, pray to thy Father
which is in secret...*
—Matthew 6:6

After "entering in" your private closet, you are responsible to "shut the door." Shut the door! Yes, *slam* it shut if necessary! Abandon your list of things to do. Forsake your agenda. Cast aside all hindrances. Take no thought of everything you *think* you must accomplish.

Your mind must be emptied of all thought, sound, or any other distraction. Once you have shut the door, make sure it is tightly closed. It is there you will cultivate intimacy with the Father, fellowship, friendship, and the inner strength to continue running the race set before you.

Approach him boldly. Purify your heart. Ask in faith. You have your Father's undivided attention, so pour your heart out. Remember, "Neither is there any creature that is not manifest in his sight: but all things are naked and opened unto the eyes of him with whom we have to do" (Hebrews 4:13).

Notes

You may wonder, "What are the consequences of not "entering in" and "shutting your door?"

You will miss friendship with the Father and the absence of his personal message to you through his Word. Often our hearts become cold and our prayers become repetitive and old. Spiritual stagnancy and dryness creep into our lives. Therefore, we must enter in and shut the door!

Chapter 7

Kingdom Living

But I say unto you which hear, Love your enemies, do good to them which hate you, Bless them that curse you, and pray for them which despitefully use you. —Luke 6:27–28

As a pastor's wife, it was difficult to watch my husband come under attack and be mistreated by the very people he poured his life into. I was aware of John 15:18, wherein Christ said,

If the world hate you, ye know that it hated me before it hated you.

And then there is also Matthew 5:11–12:

Blessed are ye, when men shall revile you, and persecute you, and shall say all manner of evil against you falsely, for my sake. Rejoice, and be exceedingly glad...

Notes

Yet, despite what I knew to be truth, I ran to my Father with my face to the ground and tears streaming.

How, O God, do you want me to respond to these people you have given into our care?

Scripture is always crystal clear, never foggy! The Holy Spirit led me to Luke 6:27–35.

> *Love your enemies. Do good to those who hate you. Bless those who curse you. Pray for those who despitefully use you. Be merciful, judge not condemn not, and forgive!*

Forgive means three little words: "let it go!"

This is Kingdom living! Anyone can love those who love them, but the mark of a child of God is the supernatural ability to love even one's enemies. This is what sets you and me apart from unbelievers. We display unity and love among the saints—the people of God.

This is what will speak the Gospel to those who sit in darkness without the hope of Christ.

Chapter 8

Rightly Loving Our Husbands

Wives, submit yourselves unto your own husbands, as unto the Lord. For the husband is the head of the wife, even as Christ is the head of the church: and he is the saviour of the body. Therefore as the church is subject unto Christ, so let the wives be to their own husbands in every thing.
—Ephesians 5:22-24

The first principle in rightly loving your husband must be borne out of your willingness to embrace God's divine order for man. First Corinthians 11:3 states,

But I would have you know that the head of every man is Christ; the head of woman is the man; and the head of Christ is God.

Therefore, we have the order: God, Christ, man, and woman. This does not mean that women are treated as inferiors, for man and woman were created equal. Once

Notes

we embrace the divine order, we are able to function within our God-given design.

The apostle Paul began his teaching about submission among believers in the body of Christ in Ephesians 5:21. Christians, in humility, are to regard others as better than themselves and lovingly serve one another. This mutual submission is the foundation for all other relationships.

And then we dig into verses 22-24 in search of the wife's responsibility: submission.

Regardless of a husband's spiritual condition, a wife is commanded to submit. This is not to be confused with the word obey as children are to do with a parent. Nor is the husband to demand it. Submission is an attitude of the heart wherein a wife willingly and lovingly lines up under the headship of her spouse. Why? Out of honor, love, and obedience to God.

Today's world has so twisted and perverted the meaning of submission that women everywhere refuse to accept it as their role. So I pray that your heart may be like clay, willing to drink deeply and fill yourselves up with God's unchanging truth!

Chapter 9

Rightly Loving Our Children

Hear, O Israel: The Lord our God is one Lord: And thou shalt love the Lord thy God with all thine heart, with all thy soul, and with all thy might. And these words, which I command thee this day, shall be in thine heart: And thou shalt teach them diligently unto thy children,and shalt talk of them when thou sittest in thinehouse, and when thou walkest by the way, and when thou liest down, and when thou risest up.
—Deuteronomy 6:4-7

If we, as women, thirst for and desire the very heart of God in all things, we shall be filled to overflowing! He gives you and me instruction in every area of life resulting in abundant joy.

We are reminded in Deuteronomy 6 that the Word of the Lord must first be in our own hearts as we love the Lord with our all. Then, we must love our children enough to nurture and teach them in the ways of the

Lord. Scripture is clear! All day long, as we walk with our children, our lips should be filled with the teaching, and the goodness and greatness of God.

The command given to you and me is "you shall teach them diligently!" The Hebrew word for diligently is *sanan*. It means with intensity, to sharpen or pierce![1]

What a responsibility we carry in passing on to the next generation a deep reverence and love for God! But it does not stop there.

If you and I are to rightly love our children, we must also express that love in three other ways:

1. We must not only teach them, but we must also discipline them. The Bible calls it the "rod of correction" (Proverbs 22:15). Proverbs is abundant with the warning of neglecting discipline. Take time to read the following verses: Proverbs 22:6, 13:24, 19:18, 22:15, and 29:15, 17. Do you want your children to be a joy to you? Read Proverbs 10:1, 23:24–25.
2. You and I must display a reverence for our husband, their father. Displaying the husband-wife relationship depicted in Ephesians 5:22–23 before your children will magnify the glory of the Father. Following your husband's leadership with a loving attitude teaches them God's intent for marriage.
3. When mothers are obedient to Titus 2:4–5, being an example of a homemaker or "keeper of the home," they cultivate an orderly, loving, peaceful and joyful haven for everyone in the household.

God's purpose is for all things to be always for his glory and in his name! Titus 2:5 tells us, that "the Word of God be not blasphemed." Fulfilling our God-given design by behaving in godly conduct was intended for you and me to display honor to the Father and his Word that the unbelieving world might look on and believe.

---

1 Warren Baker and Eugene Carpenter, The Complete Word Study Dictionary: Old Testament, AMG Publishers: Chattanooga, October 2003, p.1179.

Chapter 10

Wasted Opportunities

The aged women likewise, that they be in behaviour as becometh holiness, not false accusers, not given to much wine, teachers of good things; that they may teach the young women to be sober, to love their husbands, to love their children, To be discreet, chaste, keepers at home, good, obedient to their own husbands, that the word of God be not blasphemed.
—Titus 2:3–5

What a responsibility given to the older women in the body of Christ! As examples of godliness, they are called out to instruct the younger women in the church. (I know in America this has become a lost ministry.)

Keeping and managing a godly home with a deep reverence and respect for one's husband and children is not an option. Those who have been chiseled and shaped by life's trials, who have lived a life of abiding in him with enduring faith, are urged to pass on to the younger women their wisdom and devotion to God.

Why? It is because all we do in this life is for the glory of God. The last words of verse 5—"that the Word of God be not blasphemed"—support this answer. Exemplifying godly conduct is necessary so that the Word of God will not be dishonored. If we claim to be Christian, we must walk as Christ walked. To do otherwise is to bring reproach on scripture and the name of God.

Ladies, do not waste opportunities! Look around you and take note of those younger women who approach you for prayer and godly advice. Instruct them in the ways of the Lord, and know that in doing so, God is honored.

May you be willing to teach and lead that one who needs your wisdom and, more importantly, God's truth. It is up to the older women to teach the younger ones how to love their husbands and how to love their children while being keepers of the home. So stay alert and see who is in need of your wisdom!

Chapter 11

Spiritual Growth

But his delight is in the law of the Lord; and in his law doth he meditate day and night. And he shall be like a tree planted by the rivers of water, that bringeth forth his fruit in his season; his leaf also shall not wither; and whatsoever he doeth shall prosper.
—Psalm 1:2–3

Traveling around the world, I have found that many do not have the privilege of possessing a copy of the Word of God. They must depend upon the "hearing" of the Word, and through that hearing, they "hide" it in their hearts.

In America, we are almost casual about our Bibles. Many within the body of Christ do not even bother to remove them from the shelf, dust them off, and carry them along to the church house. So what about opening their Bibles Mondays through Saturdays?

All scripture is God-breathed. When scripture speaks, God does as well! When we yield to it and walk in obedience, it transforms our lives into the reflection of God. It is in this act of obeying that we become like Christ. Our walk and our talk do not contradict; our behavior mirrors the Word of truth. Others witness it and know that we are different. Our hearts display the fruits of repentance, and we are completely set apart unto God.

This process of spiritual growth is called sanctification. Christ prayed this in John 17:17: "Sanctify them through thy truth: thy word is truth."

The apostle Paul urges us in Romans 12:2,"And be not conformed to this world: but be ye transformed by the renewing of your mind..." The word *transformed* carries the meaning of "metamorphosis." When we renew our minds in the Word of God and meditate upon it, we are transformed!

That transformation is like a worm to a butterfly or a tadpole to a frog. We are radically changed!

As Christians, we desire Christlikeness. Therefore, we ought to hunger and thirst for righteousness, study the Word of truth, and walk in absolute obedience!

Chapter 12

The Golden Rule

And as ye would that men should do to you, do ye also to them likewise. —Luke 6:31

How many of us take the time to ponder the teaching in Luke 6:31? In his fallen state, man is completely self-absorbed. He is incapable of the sacrificial love Christ commands of all his believers. But the one who is born again and indwelt by the Holy Spirit possesses the supernatural ability to love others beyond measure.

Galatians 5:22 teaches us that love is the first fruit of the Spirit. Meanwhile, John 13:34 reminds us, "A new commandment I give unto you, That ye love one another; as I have loved you, that ye also love one another." Selfless love means serving others in the way you like to be served.

Meditate on the following questions:

1. Do I serve others with joy, kindness, and excellence just as I enjoy being served in that manner?

2. Do I build others up in my conversation as I would love to be built up and encouraged?

3. Do I express compassion toward others battling trials as I would love people to do toward me?

4. Do I pray for others as I know they are praying for my circumstances?

Romans 12:10 speaks: "Be kindly affectioned one to another with brotherly love; in honour preferring one another..." You and I are to be devoted to one another as though we were family with the blessings and grace of unconditional love. Only the Holy Spirit can empower us to love this way.

Whether I am in my own surroundings with family members, at a grocery line with strangers, in the marketplace or in the house of God with co-members of the body, I am to always treat others in the exact same way that I would like to be treated.

May our love for one another be unfeigned and fervent (1 Peter 1:22).

Part III

The Great Shepherd of the Old Testament

Now the man Moses was very meek, above all men which were upon the
face of the earth. —Numbers 12:3

Moses led six hundred thousand men. The first count in Numbers 2:32 put the figure at 603,550; and after forty years or so, it was 601,730, according to Numbers 26:51. The Levites were not actually numbered on either count though—and the figures just represented the men. If we were to multiply either figure by at least five (say an average family is a man, his wife, and three children), we would have over three million people (give or take a few thousand) in Moses's congregation!

When that is taken to heart, there is little doubt that Moses was the greatest shepherd of all time (that is, besides the Lord). David is considered the shepherd of Israel; but the application is as a king, not as a minister. Though David was undoubtedly a prophet, there is a distinction between serving as king and being the intercessor and preacher for a congregation that filled the Sinai wilderness.

Moses wrote the law—the first five books of the Old Testament (The book of Job is attributed to him as well as Psalm 90). The people murmured against him ten times; they rebelled and wanted to stone him—even his own sister led a revolt against the great shepherd of Israel! Still, there is no pastor in the history of man that compares to Moses. Although he was a reluctant servant, he was a faithful one.

We know the heart of Moses from these lines:

Yet now, if thou wilt forgive their sin—; and if not, blot me, I pray thee, out of
thy book which thou hast written. (Exodus 32:32)

And he said, I beseech thee, shew me thy glory. (Exodus 33:18)

Here is why he is the greatest shepherd next to the Good and Great Shepherd, the bishop of our souls:

1. Moses delivered the very Word of God and his commandments (Exodus 20:1–21). He revealed the character of God in good judgment and loving kindness.
2. He was an intercessor for people who treated him with contempt (Exodus 32:30). The man loved his people even when they gave him every reason not to.
3. Moses did signs and wonders, and yet he was meek and took no glory (Exodus 34:7–12). He is compared to Elijah, Elisha, Jesus, and the apostles.
4. He spent forty days and nights on Mt. Sinai two times with no food and water (Exodus 24:18; 34:28). No man can do that without the sustaining presence of God.
5. Moses is also compared to Christ, who would come as a Prophet (Deuteronomy 18:15; 18–19). There is no higher compliment on earth!
6. He was buried by God on Mount Nebo (where the Lord showed Moses the Promised Land) because he served so well (Deuteronomy 34:5–7). Michael the archangel and the devil fought over his body (Jude 9).

Part IV

An Overview of Sound Doctrine

Chapter 1

The Infallibility of Scripture

The Bible is infallible in its original form. Though there are no copies of the original texts, God has been fully able to preserve his truth through every generation just as he totally inspired it. The scripture is altogether reliable, meets the test of time, and has been confirmed by archaeological discoveries. Christians will always place unchanging biblical truth above ever-changing science.

This is essential because the Bible is the authority in faith and practice. Christian leaders are called on as Gospel preachers to proclaim the Word of God in the proper context and to teach the people of God to submit to the scriptures and to order their lives, families, and churches by biblical truth. It is never enough to merely know the truth; Christians must also be true examples before the world.

Here are scriptural texts that affirm the Word of God:

- Joshua 1:8

- Psalm 12:6, 19:7–11

- Isaiah 55:11

- Matthew 5:17–18, 24:35

- John 17:17

- Romans 10:17, 16:25–26

- Ephesians 6:17

- Colossians 3:16

- 2 Timothy 3:15-17, 4:2-4

- Hebrews 4:12

- James 1:21-22

- 2 Peter 1:20-21

The Word calls Christians to be ever ready to give affirmation to the miracles of the Bible (especially the virgin birth and the resurrection), the reality of heaven and hell, the fallen nature of man, the penalty of sin, the coming of the Lord Jesus as God in the flesh, the second coming of Jesus as the Lord of all, and the undeniable truth that he is the only savior of the world.

Notes

Chapter 2

The Work of the Church

The church is to be the glory of God on the earth. The Bible describes the church three ways in the New Testament: The bride of Christ, the body of Christ, and a spiritual building. The church is led by pastors (elders and/or bishops) and served by deacons. Revivalists (the prophetic gift), missionaries (the apostolic gift), evangelists (gifted soul winners and harvesters), and Bible teachers are also essential to the church's leadership and development.

(Note: No one has the authority to add revelation to the Word of God. No Bible teacher has the level of inspiration as the prophets and apostles who God used to give us the Word of God.)

A church is not just a Bible study group but a people committed to fulfilling the Great Commission led by biblical leadership. For a church to be legitimate, it must follow the doctrine of Christ and the apostles—to be as close to the New Testament belief and practice as possible. The ordinances of the church are baptism by immersion and administration of the Lord's Table—where the bread and fruit of the vine are served, representing the broken body and shed blood of Jesus.

Here are biblical references of support:

- Ephesians 5:25–27, Revelation 19:7–9

- 1 Corinthians 12:12–27, Ephesians 4:11–16

- 1 Peter 2:4–8

- 1 Timothy 3:1-15, Titus 1:5-9

- Matthew 28:17-20, Mark 16:15-16, Luke 24:47-48, John 20:21, Acts 1:8

- Ephesians 2:20, Hebrews 4:12, James 1:21-22

- Matthew 3:13-17, Romans 6:3-5, Colossians 2:12

- Matthew 26:26-30, 1 Corinthians 11:17-34

The church is called to submit to biblical authority, to operate in love for one another and love for the lost, and to worship the Lord in spirit and truth. The church services are not performances and stage productions, but they are where the people serve the Lord and one another for an audience of One. The work of the church is ultra practical— meeting needs, but most of all, the need for salvation and discipleship, strong family life, and missions support.

Notes

Chapter 3

The Biblical Model of Family Life

The Creator made each man one woman to love for a lifetime. His intent was for them to have a holy union and produce godly offspring. He placed the altar before the bed. Premarital sex and extramarital sex are no less wicked and damning offenses. He hates divorce and does not excuse it as a guise for adultery. Christians and Christian leaders, especially, are to be examples of purity, faithfulness, and godliness in family life.

- Genesis 3:24, Ephesians 5:21-33

- Malachi 2:14-16

- Hebrews 13:4

- Galatians 5:19-21, Ephesians 5:5, 1 Thessalonians 4:3

- 1 Timothy 3:1-15, 6:11-12; Titus 1:5-16, 2:11-14

- 1 Peter 3:1-7

- Colossians 3:18-21

- 1 Corinthians 7:1-40

- Proverbs 18:22, 31:10-31

The husband and wife are to give themselves to each another in love, not defraud each other. They should take care of their appearance to keep the fires of love and romance burning so that the world has no grip on the soul of their marriage partner. The Lord makes a man for a woman, a woman for a man; he has our match.

The man is the spiritual leader and he has great accountability. He will one day present his family before the Lord. Fathers should show their sons and daughters how to protect and provide for the home. Mothers are to make their home a haven of peace for the father, her husband, and the children. The father is the head of the home while the mother is the heart.

The first priority of the home should be scripture and prayer. The key is to serve the Lord first and then the marriage. The children are not to be prioritized over everything else (except when their care requires immediate attention).

Notes

Chapter 4

The Commissions of Jesus

The Lord left five commissions for his church that serve as his last will and testament—these are his directives for all true believers until he comes again. No church is complete in obedience without making disciples, baptizing believers, and taking the Gospel to all unreached people. Each of these commissions has something to say about the church's priorities.

The commissions of the Lord Jesus are found in each Gospel and in the first chapter of the Acts:

- Matthew 28:18–20

- Mark 16:15–18

- Luke 24:47–48

- John 20:21

- Acts 1:8

Matthew's Gospel is the most comprehensive. It has a mandate to spread the Gospel among all nations.

Mark's commission is the most direct, calling on the church to take the message to every creature. It includes a reference to the supernatural.

Luke's Gospel calls on Christians to preach repentance among all nations.

John has the most succinct rendering.

The commission in Acts speaks of power, the Holy Spirit, and the charge to be witnesses—from the home city, to the region, to the nation, and then to the uttermost part of the earth.

So why are there five versions of the commission of Jesus?

When the Lord repeated something, it meant that it was essential. Yet there are too few churches today that take the Master's clear instructions to heart. They need to be reminded that those five passages are the Lord's mandate for the church.

Notes

Chapter 5

Regeneration and Salvation

Salvation can come only after the Lord has regenerated the heart. No one can come to the Lord unless he draws him or her to himself. Salvation from beginning to end is the work of God. When a person is saved, it is a revolution of the heart: old things are passed away, and all things become new (2 Corinthians 5:17). The very presence of God indwells the believer.

- Titus 3:5

- John 6:44; 65

- Ephesians 2:8-10

- 2 Corinthians 5:17

- 1 John 3:24

Salvation does not come and go. Once the Lord saves a soul from sin, hell, and death, it is for keeps. Salvation cannot be lost once people are regenerated. That, however, does not mean that professing believers can do whatever they want and still be saved. When salvation comes, believers will repent, turn away from sin, and live for Jesus. There is no truth in a life that claims the Savior but continues in sin.

- John 10:27-29

- Philippians 1:6

- Ephesians 1:13

- Hebrews 12:2

- Jude 24

- 1 John 3:7–10, 5:13, 18

Salvation is not a matter of praying a sinner's prayer and then being baptized. Jesus taught that "Narrow is the way, which leadeth unto life, and few there be that find it" (Matthew 7:14). Salvation is evident with a changed life, selflessness, and a heart given to service. John declared that people of saving faith cannot love the world and love the Lord (1 John 2:15–17), and James affirmed the same truth (James 4:4).

Notes

115

Chapter 6

The Holy Spirit

The Holy Spirit of God is first noted in scripture in Genesis 1:2 as he moved upon the face of the waters at creation. He came upon men to prophesy in the Old Testament. The Bible teaches God as Father, Son, and Holy Spirit—three in one. God is omnipresent. He can be in more than one place at a time. Those who dismiss this misunderstand the nature of God.

The Holy Spirit indwells men in the New Testament. He seals them for the day of redemption. He endows them with spiritual gifts. He teaches them all things that Jesus has commanded of us. He was the inspiration of the Word of God—from Genesis to Revelation. We are baptized by the Holy Spirit once and filled with the Spirit of God repeatedly. The Spirit of God is God.

Biblical references on the person and work of the Holy Spirit:

- Matthew 28:19

- John 14:16–17, 26–27

- John 16:13

- Acts 5:3–4, 32

- Romans 8

- Ephesians 1:13, 6:17

- Titus 3:5

- Jude 20

The Holy Spirit of God can be grieved (Ephesians 4:30) and quenched (1 Thessalonians 5:19). The context of grieving the Holy Spirit of God is in the use of words. The quenching of the Holy Spirit is through an attitude of ingratitude, the denial of his power, and an absence of a spirit of prayer. Without the Spirit, people cannot belong to the Lord (Romans 8:9, 1 John 3:24).

Notes

Chapter 7

Spiritual Gifts

There are three passages that identify the gifts of the Spirit. The gifts are the endowments of God for all believers. The lists of gifts are not exhaustive. But it's important to remember that Christians must seek *God* and not the gifts. There is a difference between natural and supernatural gifts—supernatural gifts are spiritual, God given. Jesus had all the gifts, whereas, no Christian has them all, so believers need one another.

Here are the biblical references on spiritual gifts: Romans 12, 1 Corinthians 12, and Ephesians 4:8–16.

There have been times in the history of man when the Lord has shown signs and wonders through prophets and apostles. Those times are distinct: the days of Moses and Joshua, the years of Elijah and Elisha, and the time of Christ and the apostles. Isolated miracles occurred throughout time, but there were no other ages of true signs and wonders. Yet God can do his wonders as he will, but it is always to his glory and praise, and in keeping with his Word.

All gifts should be used in the context of the church according to biblical instructions. Many so-called gifts today have nothing to do with the context of scripture, and much of what happens has no foundation in New Testament life. Satan will counterfeit and do lying wonders. The accuser of the brethren can work his deception in the church and multiply error.

References on error and deception in the church:

- 2 Corinthians 11:13–15

- 1 Timothy 4:1–3

- 2 Timothy 3:1–5

- 2 Peter 2:1–3

- 1 John 4:1

Churches debate whether or not the spiritual gifts of miracles, healings, and tongues continued beyond the first century. Many cults and Christian groups claim these gifts, but few (if any) are used in the context of scripture. Many of those who claim to be filled with the Holy Spirit and exercise these gifts are, unfortunately, immoral and unethical.

The scripture is the final authority for all faith and practice—not personal experience. Gifts were given to authenticate the apostles' ministry and authority in their time. In our time, they are given to authenticate the Word of God. In the last days, deception and delusion will intensify, and false signs and wonders will multiply (Mark 13:22, Rev.13:11–15).

Many contemporary practices have no reference in the New Testament.

Speaking in Tongues

Speaking in tongues has been one of the most divisive issues in the church. Most of the time, when tongues are used in the church today, they are not in the context of the scripture, and no interpretation of tongues usually follows that is anything more than just a spiritual generality. Many churches given to tongues admit that they are not speaking an actual language but "the tongues of angels."

First Corinthians 13:1 is a reference to eloquence, not a private prayer language. First Corinthians 14:19 speaks to 10,000 words in an "unknown tongue"—that is, a tongue not known by the speaker, not a tongue unknown among all men. There is little evidence for a universal prayer language in the early church or in the church today (1 Corinthian 14:14–15).

The Bible does say in 1 Corinthians 14:39, "...Forbid not to speak with tongues," though the church is to forbid tongues when they are taken out of the biblical context

Notes

and when it causes confusion. Speaking in tongues and the interpretation of tongues, when it was a common practice in the church, was listed as the last of the spiritual gifts.

Here are the biblical references:

- Mark 16:17; Acts 2:3-13, 10:46, 19:6

- 1 Corinthians 12:10, 28, 30; 13:1, 8; 14:1-40

Principles from the New Testament:

1. When the Holy Ghost came, they did not always speak in tongues (Acts 3:1, 4:22).
2. Tongues were a known language (Acts 2:8).
3. When Peter preached at Pentecost, he did not even reference tongues (Acts 2:14, 40).
4. The word for tongues in 1 Corinthians 14:2 and in Acts is the same. The context speaks to a known language although unknown to the speaker.
5. All tongues used in the church assembly must have interpretation (1 Corinthians 14:5, 13, 26-28).
6. Women were not to speak in tongues (1 Corinthians 14:34).
7. The call throughout the biblical text on tongues (1 Corinthians 14) was to give preference to prophesy, not tongues.
8. It is stated in 1 Corinthians 14:4, 23-25 that tongues did not edify the church or the lost without interpretation, but prophesy always did.

Remember that the Corinthian church was not a model church. They were full of immorality and error. Believers should not follow the broken example of the Corinthians. In charismatic churches, most tongue speakers are women. But the admonition forbids them from speaking. It can be a learned behavior, typical among cults, the occult, and world religions.

Chapter 8

New Testament Giving

The Old Testament had definite teaching on tithes and offerings. There were two tithes to be given each year and another every three years (23.3 percent). The New Testament affirms the practice of giving tithes in the teaching of Jesus, but grace always supersedes the law. Gifts that come from the heart of worship never fall short of gifts that are required. Giving is what Christians do.

Here are biblical references on tithes and offerings:

- Genesis 14:18–20

- Exodus 36:3–7

- Leviticus 27:30

- Deuteronomy 12:6; 14:22, 28–29; 16:10, 16–17

- 1 Chronicles 29:2–14

So there were tithes on the land and livestock (10 percent), the festival tithes (10 percent), and the tithes set for every three years (3 percent). The last was the "poor tithe" to support the Levite, the stranger, the fatherless, and the widow. Then the Hebrews added to this their free-will offerings! (Matthew 23:23 and Luke 11:42 confirm the standard of the tithe.)

The following are New Testament references on giving:

- Acts 2:45, 4:33–35, 20:35

- Romans 12:13

- 2 Corinthians 8:2–5, 9:6–15

- Philippians 4:15–18

- 1 Peter 4:8–10

Christians are stewards of all that the Lord puts in their hands. The churches of the Acts were quite different from the churches of today: there were no monies spent on lands and buildings. There were no big budgets. The early Christians gave about 90 percent of their offerings to reach others and meet their needs. But today we give an average of about 10 percent.

Chapter 9

True Worship

Jesus was the first to raise the question of true worship in John 4. He did what was unheard of in that day: he spoke to a woman of ill repute at Jacob's well in Samaria—he had much to say.

Here is the summary of the conversation:

1. The place of worship is not the primary concern but how people worship.

2. Worship the Father through Jesus by the power of the Spirit of God.

3. Worship is only acceptable when it is done in spirit and in truth.

4. The Father seeks that kind of worship and those kinds of worshippers.

The Bible is definitive about the need for worship. God longs for us to get it right and to be right. All have a longing for worship, but most seek to satisfy it with false worship and idolatry. All is right when men worship the true and Living God.

Notes

True worship is God-centered and never man-centered. It is Christ exalting. Biblical worship included praise, thanksgiving, prayers, intercession, exhortation, and expository messages from the scriptures.

Here are references on worship in the Bible:

- Genesis 4:4, 22:12

- Exodus 3:2-5, 33:8-23

- Joshua 5:13-15, 24:15

- Job 42:1-6

- Psalm 19:7-14; 26:8; 27:4, 8; 46:10; 51:17; 63:1-4; 67:1-7; 73:24-26; 84:4-5, 10-12; 95:6-8; 96:6-9; 100:1-4; 113:3-6; 115:1; 118:21-24; 119:9-11, 18, 38, 47, 89, 97, 105, 160; 130:3-5; 133:1-3; 134:1-3; 139:1-18, 23-24; 150:1-6

- Isaiah 6:1-8

- Habakkuk 2:20, 3:2; Zephaniah 3:17

- Malachi 1:11; 3:2-3, 10, 16

- Matthew 8:23-27

- Luke 18:9-14, 21:1-4

- Acts 4:31, 7:55-60

- Ephesians 3:14-21

- Hebrews 12:22-29

- Jude 24-25

- Revelation 1:12-18, 5:9-14, 7:9-17, 19:5-10

When the people of God fight over styles of music, they have missed the point of worship. It is not about man but God! It is not about personal preferences. It is about the glory of God. Worship brings the people of God before his throne so that his presence is known and reverence fills the soul of man.

Chapter 10

Historic Christian Faith

No church or denomination can trace a direct line back to Christ and the apostles. Churches may claim that status; but few churches operate with the simplicity, generosity, and all-out evangelism and missions of the early church.

What is historic Christian faith? It is the Gospel in terms set apart from church property and buildings, icons and images, and the commandments of men that have nothing to do with what Jesus and his men taught or how they lived. They were simple men who took the death, burial, and resurrection of Jesus to the nations with much sacrifice and little fanfare.

Here are the historic principles of the Christian faith:

1. We are justified by faith alone in the Lord Jesus (Romans 1:17, Galatians 3:11, Hebrews 10:38).
2. The truth of scriptures is the basis of faith and not the traditions of men (Mark 7:1-13, 2 Timothy 3:15-17, Hebrews 4:12, 2 Peter 1:20-21).
3. The church is governed by elders and served by deacons under Christ (1 Timothy 3:1-13; Titus 1:5-9; Hebrews 13:7, 17).

4. Believers are baptized by immersion as a testimony of the death, burial, and resurrection of Jesus and a sign of lifelong devotion to him (Matthew 3:13-17, 28:19; Romans 6:3-5).
5. The Lord's Table represents the broken body and shed blood of Jesus (Matthew 26:26-30; 1 Corinthians 10:21,11:17-34).
6. The church is called to disciple all nations as we lift up Jesus as Lord (Matthew 28:19; Luke 24:47; Acts 1:8; Rom. 1:5, 16:26).
7. Genuine believers live the Christian life by grace and the power of the Holy Spirit (Acts 5:32, Romans 8:14, Eph. 2:8-10, Titus 3:4-7).
8. Christians live not unto themselves but to the glory and praise of God (Romans 5:2, 14:7-8, 15:5-7; 1 Corinthians 1:29, 31).

What is the historic Gospel of Christ?

It is the repentance of all known sins and placing faith in Christ alone to save us from sin, death, and hell.

Many churches depart from the sacred scriptures for worldly expediency. They bring into the church beliefs that have no basis in New Testament life. As a result, most churches are not operating according to the Bible. Today there is little concern about sound doctrine and godly living. Church leadership has been redefined. So-called conversion requires little commitment.

Historic Christian faith lives out the teachings of Jesus and practices the principles of the New Testament so that the church has a viable witness. The true church makes the Lord look good because his glory is made known.

Chapter 11

Church Discipline

Church discipline has been lost for the last few generations. As a result, many churches have lost the Gospel message that delivers men from sin. There were many flaws in the churches of New Testament times, yet when we compare the church of the Acts and epistles to those in the present day, without a doubt, none compare to the "anything goes" mind-set of the church today!

People think they can believe anything they want to believe in, act in any way they want to act, come as little as they want to come, give practically nothing, yet still be considered members of the church. They can be critical, hateful, divisive, and bona fide gossips and do absolutely nothing to serve Jesus but still be a member of the church in good standing.

This is a mockery of scripture, the Lord Jesus, and the Gospel. The epistles deal with false teaching and corrective action so that the church could be kept true and pure. The evidence in the New Testament is overwhelming: godly leadership in the first age of the church meant having the courage to call the people to holiness and righteousness.

Note the following references, among many, for church discipline in the New Testament:

- Matthew 18:15–25, Luke 17:1–4

127

- Acts 5:1–11, 8:4–25; Romans 16:17–18; 1 Corinthians 5:1, 6:20

- Galatians 5:19–21, 6:1; Ephesians 5:5–7; Philippians 3:17–19; 2 Thessalonians 3:6–12; 1 Timothy 1:19–20, 4:1–3; 2 Timothy 3:1–9

- Hebrews 10:22–31; James 2:1–9; 1 Peter 4:17; 2 Peter 2:1–3, 12–22

- 2 John 1:9–11; 3 John 1:9–11; Jude 10–13, 16

- Revelation 2:4–5, 14–16, 20–23; 3:2–3, 15–19

The loss of church discipline means that the church has become apostate. When church leaders can act unbecoming to the Gospel of Christ, then members will be more inclined to do so too. Often it starts with compromised leadership in family and marriage, finances, and ethical matters. The lack of biblical standards in the home and church all come from the failure to practice sound doctrine.

When church discipline is put in place, it should be done graciously along the lines of Matthew 18:15–35. Also, keep in mind the admonition in Galatians 6:1. The goal of church discipline is restoration to the fellowship. When there is repentance (turning away from sin), then the church must forgive—though church leaders can be disqualified, if they're no longer examples of the faith.

Chapter 12

Prophecy

One of the joys of digging deep into the scripture is to know what the Lord has promised for the future. There are many books that are considered prophetic and speak to our age and generation. These are but a few:

- Ezekiel

- Daniel

- Joel

- Zechariah

- Matthew

- Luke

- Romans

- 1 Thessalonians

- 2 Thessalonians

- 1 Timothy

- 2 Timothy

Notes

- 2 Peter

- 1 John

- Jude

- Revelation

Perspectives on prophecy are diverse. Luke 12:35 tells churches the kind of viewpoint all believers should hold. There is no definite blueprint laid out, but there are major revelations about what will come and how to be ready.

What is essential for believers is to take the Gospel into neighborhoods and nations, not debate the nitty-gritty of prophecy. Acts 1:11 tells the church not to be "gazing up into heaven" but to get blazing the glad tidings until he comes!

Here is a pre-millennial, pre-tribulation view of prophecy:

1. The time of the Gentiles will conclude with the coming of the Lord for his Church in clouds of glory (Romans 11:25, 1 Thessalonians 4:13–18).

2. The Lord will turn his face back to his people, the Jews. Israel will be saved. They will become a believing people (Romans 11:26, Zechariah 12:10).

3. During both eras, the Holy Spirit will redeem both Gentile and Jew as he sees fit (Romans 10:8, 11:12).

4. There will be seven years of tribulation on earth under the rule of the Anti-Christ (Daniel 9:24–27, Matt. 24:3–51).

5. The Lord will return to the earth and set his feet on the Mount of Olives when he rescues his people and fights the battle of Armageddon (Zephaniah 3:8; Zechariah 14:1–17; Rev. 14:14–20, 19:11–21).

6. The Anti-Christ and the false prophet will be cast into the lake of fire, and Satan will be bound for a thousand years (Rev. 19:19, 20:3).

7. The Lord will reign upon the earth for a thousand years with Jerusalem as his international capital (Isaiah 65:17–25, Revelation 20:4–6).

8. At the end of the millennium, the last battle will occur when Satan is "loosed out of his prison"—so that all who are in the flesh will determine their allegiance—be quickly defeated and then cast into the lake of fire (Revelation 20:7–10).

The rebirth of Israel on May 14, 1948, was not happenstance but providence. Though the nation came back secular, it will one day turn to the God of Abraham, Isaac, and Jacob—and know that Jesus is Lord and Messiah!

Notes

Part V

Twelve Principles of Christian Leadership

There are hundreds of volumes and perspectives written on leadership, many of them more in tune with successful business and/or cultural models than in line with God's design as found in the Bible. These principles come from the refining fires of church planting and shepherding churches from zero to a few hundred. Ministry is much more than a profession. True ministry is a calling from God. He gives what we need in wisdom, gifting, and perseverance to serve the people of God.

1. In staff relations and key church leadership, loyalty to the lead pastor is essential and cannot be compromised without causing discord.
2. Church economics is altogether different from how the world operates.

   a. It costs money to minister to people, and the returns are not always sure.
   b. Christians live responsibly, are without debt, and never factor out faith.
   c. If a church fails to meet the budget, the answer is not to make cuts in the budget but to increase prayer.
   d. A budget should reflect what God has called the church to do in ministry.
   e. It should place priority on evangelism, discipleship, and missions.
   f. The church should be a model of generosity, sacrifice, and stewardship.
   g. Full-time pastors should be compensated. The Bible says that they are worthy of double honor. But they are not to be lovers of money.
   h. Money can be a snare of the devil. It is best to let the people handle the funds under the guidance of the pastors so that all may be accountable.

3. Learn true generosity, and couple it with discernment of the Spirit. There are many beggars in the church and many worthy causes that exclude the mission of the church. Church worship services should not be fund-raising events.
4. Be careful not to beat a dead horse. That means you shouldn't do the same thing over and over with few fruits. Stay fresh and be sure that every event and expenditure is God honoring and has a biblical basis.
5. Be assured that all Bible teachers are sound in the faith, faithful in their witness, examples in the community, and that they actually teach the Bible in class.
6. Start discipleship early on with children so that they know the Bible, develop a Christian worldview, and are able to defend their faith.
7. Expect your church leaders to be diligent, gracious, faithful to services, tithers, active in evangelism, discipleship, and missions. If they are not faithful and full of faith, they should not be church leaders.
8. Guard worship services against unending announcements, pointless testimonies, frivolity, immodesty, and excessive emotionalism.
9. Understand that pettiness, murmurings, and a critical spirit are the devil's currency. Do not give way to such ungodly character traits in the fellowship.
10. Give no place to anyone who says, "Not everyone is called to evangelism and missions." It is proof that they do not know their Bibles or the Great Commission of Jesus. In fact, all are called to evangelism and missions!

11. Teach your people to be Christian servants who think little of themselves but much of Christ and precious souls. People who come to the church should be served well—with excellence and a good attitude.
12. In selecting leaders and receiving members, teach them the abiding principle based on John 15:1–17. In order to be fruitful, they must stay connected to the Lord with daily Bible time and prayer.

- They need to have a close walk with God and a lifestyle of repentance.
- The people should know what it means to "practice the presence of God," so that they "live near the flame of God" and have clean hearts.
- Abiding means tenacity, perseverance, and steadfastness.
- When the people are connected to the heart of God, their lives are characterized by their love for him, the church, and the lost. They're fruitful!

Notes

135

Part VI

Christian Leadership Training

The intent of these lessons is to teach men of God to start new churches wherever people meet. New churches do not have a high survival rate, but viability can be increased with good training. This is designed to be an on-the- frontlines seminary to give an overview of the Bible and of Christian ministry.

There are instructions on how to set up a church planting school. The authors have had six and three years of seminary respectively. These lessons are distilled and very condensed versions of the courses students would take in a Bible college-and-seminary setting.

The church planting school has two parts: Doctrine Studies and Christian Leadership Training. The school is to be taught on a twelve-month time frame. It is best to utilize the lessons as a starting point of healthy interaction from the students so that questions can be asked and answered.

Introduction: Biblical Church Planting

1. Bible Interpretation

2. Bible Preaching

3. Church Planting

4. The Old Testament Law, History, Wisdom, and Prophets

5. The New Testament Gospels

6. The Acts of the Holy Spirit

7. The New Testament Epistles

8. The Revelation of Jesus

9. Bible Doctrines

10. Church History

11. Christian Apologetics

12. Spiritual Warfare

Instructions for Christian Leadership Training

1. This frontline seminary can offer two classes per month: one in Christian Leadership and another in Doctrine Studies as found in part IV. The two courses can be alternated or taught separately, six months at a time.
2. "Biblical Church Planting" is an introduction featuring the book of Titus to start the school. If not all students have a manual, copy the pages for that particular lesson for each student before the class begins.
3. There are twelve lessons for Christian Leadership and twelve lessons from the Doctrine Studies. The latter of the two are designed to have the students dig into the scriptures. All lessons have biblical references.
4. The goal of the church planting school is to give basic instruction in leadership and doctrine so that the students can start new churches everywhere— in homes, schools, the marketplace, and even under a tree!
5. These twenty-four studies are a starting point to equipping church planters with tools for Christian leadership. The men and women are encouraged to be like the Bereans, who searched the scriptures to see if these things were true (Acts 17:11).

Notes

139

Introduction

Biblical Church Planting

TITUS 1-3

This is the greatest way to extend the Gospel and make disciples known to man, and it is the way of the church of the Acts. The apostles went everywhere starting and establishing churches. They preached the truth, warned of error, paid the price, and traveled on to the next unreached district. The Holy Spirit led the way to making Jesus known by all means. In fact, they may have reached further in that first generation than any other has since!

Titus was a young pastor. The apostle Paul was his mentor and the writer of the book (Titus 1:1).

1. Elect elders in every city (Titus 1:5).
   Titus 1:3 reveals how Paul did his work: He preached! He encouraged Titus to elect men to preach the Word in every city. Note that there was always a plurality of leadership. Leaders were men with qualified wives who were their partners in ministry. (The list of character traits are in these verses and in 1 Timothy 3:1-7.) The church has stepped far away from the Bible. For generations, leadership has been grossly compromised. Be careful not to do that! These men were elders and not deacons. They were rulers. They were to have their families in order, for how could they rule the house of God if they could not rule their own household (1 Timothy 3:5)? They were to be men of the Word and prayer (Acts 6:4) to equip the church to do the work of ministry (Eph. 4:12). They were not to do everything themselves, but to train the people to minister God's amazing grace!

2. Speak sound doctrine (Titus 1:9)
   Note Titus 1:9, 16. The church planter's teaching is nonnegotiable. It is ordered by the Word. He must be bold enough to stand against naysayers, those who speak against Gospel action or spiritual progress. They must know that the people's profession of faith is only as good as their practice and obedience. Wise leaders constantly reproduce themselves by teaching sound doctrine and

living out the Word. In that environment, leaders develop and thrive.

3. Know the grace of God (Titus 2:11).
   We have a great definition of the Gospel message in Titus 2:11-14. Salvation is to be freely offered to all men. Salvation means denying ungodliness and worldly lusts. They are to live soberly, righteously, and godly in this world. The appearing of Jesus is that blessed hope. He has redeemed men from iniquity to purify them so that they would be zealous to do good works. This is not always the Gospel message that is heard today. When God's grace comes in, sin goes out. Sin and the Savior do not camp together!

4. Be ready to do good works (Titus 3:1).
   Take a close look at Titus 1:16; 2:7, 14; 3:1, 8, 14. What is the theme?

   The evidence of grace applied is a bounty of good works. In the final chapter, Christians learn that good works do not come from self-righteousness but from the work of the Holy Spirit in believers (Titus 3:5). Good works never save God's people, but they are a proof to the world that they are saved. Good works indicate acts of service, excellence, and righteousness.

   The greatest appeal a church has to the community is righteous conversation.

   Church planting is often mistaken for "church splits" when it's really not. It is difficult to establish a viable Gospel witness if a new church is formed because the preacher or people could not get along with the one they broke away from—that is the worst possible witness. Disunity and infighting are not inviting to the Lord or the world!

Notes

141

Chapter 1

Bible Interpretation

Study to shew thyself approved unto God, a workman that needeth not to be ashamed, rightly dividing the word of truth. —2 Timothy 2:15

There is only one correct interpretation of the Bible, and that is the Holy Spirit's. He inspired forty men to write sixty-six books, covering a span of fifteen hundred years, on three continents. The Bible is infallible and inerrant in its original form. God has preserved and protected his Word so that it is fully reliable, and it is the authority over the Christian life and the foundation of every true church.

Nehemiah 8:8 and Acts 8:30–35 reveal the role of the preacher. He helps the hearers of the Word understand what God is saying. The source of authority is not the preacher but the Word of God. The preacher has power as he reveals the truths of God's Word, which is alive and active as Hebrews 4:12 says. It cuts to the heart and discerns the thoughts and intentions of the heart.

There is only one interpretation of the scripture, but there are many ways in which it can be applied. Yet those too must be true to the intent of the Holy Spirit of God. Proper interpretation of biblical principles produces a godly lifestyle.

The Gospel preacher is faithful to the biblical background of the passage he preaches. He understands the language, the geography, the culture, the history, and the worldview at the time the passage was written.

Here are further principles of interpretation:

1. Take the literal view of the Bible and not the figurative.
    Though there are figurative passages, there are always literal applications. Be careful about going beyond what the text says. Many preachers are guilty of this!

2. Not every promise in the Bible has personal application. Many references, for example, are for

God's people, the Jews. It is essential to know who the promise is for in the context of the passage.

3. Remember that the Bible has a God-centered worldview. All that is there is for the glory and praise of the Lord. Never twist scripture to honor man or exalt the flesh. The Bible never justifies the sin or the sinner.

4. No part of the Bible contradicts another. An example is the death of Judas narrated in both Matthew 27:5 and Acts 1:18. He hung himself, and then his body fell and "burst asunder." There is an explanation for any apparent contradiction.

5. When it comes to biblical parables, there is a primary truth that is conveyed. A parable both reveals and conceals truth for those who understand. It is the Holy Spirit who makes it clear so that the meaning of the story can be told.

6. Once there is proper interpretation, personal application must follow. Teach obedience by personal example. The Bible always calls believers to action. If the text says to go and preach the Gospel, do not stay put and remain silent!

7. Know the historic interpretation of the text. How have the verses been interpreted throughout the history of the church? An example is, "What qualifies spiritual leadership?" Many times, the culture can override the text.

8. Be careful to distinguish between what is recorded in the Bible and what God approves. If ungodly behavior is recorded, it does not mean that God was honored by it. The Bible reveals consequences of sinful acts, so be forewarned.

Notes

143

Chapter 2

Bible Preaching

Preach the word; be instant in season, out of season; reprove, rebuke, ex-hort with all long suffering and doctrine. —2 Timothy 4:2

The Gospel preacher works hard: he studies, prays, and learns how to communicate clearly to the people. The work of the ministry is a spiritual battle, and it can be discouraging at times. The preacher should seek the Lord for his blessing in the gifts and skills of Christian ministry so that he becomes the bold and gracious servant of God that he ought to be.

Biblical preaching relies on the power of the Holy Spirit and seeks to change hearts and minds so that people obey the truth. It exalts the Lord, edifies the church, and expands the reach of the Gospel. It humbles men and magnifies the Lord and his mighty deeds. It adorns the doctrine of God.

The way a preacher lives his life is always louder than his words. The way he delivers the message goes much further than what he has to say—but, he does have something to say! He is not merely a teacher who adds up knowledge. He is called to transform lives by truth. The message should burn in his heart.

Principles of biblical preaching:

1. The preacher is to be called by God to preach the Word. He is to love the Lord and have a passion to serve him at all costs. The church should affirm his gifts and calling (Acts 13:1–3). The Gospel preacher must love people.

2. The Bible preacher has to know the Bible. It is his authority and foremost reference for family life, commerce, church life, and character development. The man of God is to study the entire scripture and put it into practice.

3. He must be totally aware of the spiritual battle he faces. As a preacher, he will experience it to a high degree; he will be tempted, discouraged, and tried by fire. As the pastor of a church, the battle will be all the more difficult.

4. He is to preach the text faithfully but also know the people personally. The man of God has to know where they're hurting and answer the questions they're asking. He must be strong on application and not betray confidences. The minister must also preach with both the mind and the heart.

5. The Bible is an inexhaustible resource of truth. Do not be a lighthearted and an elementary preacher. Go deep and wide with the whole counsel of God. Keep it simple but still go deep.

6. Be sure that the people get the main point of the text. Keep words to a minimum so that every word counts. Be timely so that the sermon is finished before the people are! Leave room for the Gospel invitation. Point them to Christ.

7. Use good illustrations that come from recent real-life events. Jesus was the master illustrator. Take time to tell the story, but do not become just a storyteller! Read the Bible text well; pause where pauses are needed.

8. Learn to read the people. If the Gospel preacher is going to go for the heart, he must be led by the Holy Spirit. The preacher may see people smile, weep, scowl or yawn! Facial expressions are one of the ways the people communicate back to him.

9. Keep humble. Preach for the praise of God, not men. Keep short accounts on sin with God. Do not be a hypocrite. Practice what is preach! Look people in the eye, never tear them down, but lead them in worship!

Notes

10. It has been wisely said, "Don't waste his (the Lord's) time with your jokes." That is a blow to many preachers who use humor in an effort to connect with the people, but the truth is there is no biblical pattern for joking and jesting.

Chapter 3
Church Planting

And daily in the temple, and in every house, they ceased not to teach and preach Jesus Christ..." Therefore they that were scattered abroad went every where preaching the word. —Acts 5:42, 8:4

Church planting is the best way to reach every man, to make disciples, to teach all that Jesus commanded, to baptize new believers and to keep the church fresh and filled with the Spirit. Older churches do not reach as many people, they can easily become stagnant, and turn inward. New churches have no traditions, no restrictions, and no obstacles in going after souls and reaching all kinds of people.

Principles of church planting:

1. Healthy churches grow, and a big part of growth is to reproduce churches. More than anything else, church planting can reach a community with sustained ministry. So what is a healthy church? It is one that has biblical leadership and fulfills the Great Commission of Jesus. It is a place where conflict is minimized and Gospel practice is maximized.

147

2. Here are keys in starting a new church: Pray, pray, and pray. Sow the seed of the Word of God widely. Make it a habit to share the Gospel by some means with everyone. Start small groups. Develop a team of people who will work in harmony with each other and with great faith. Set a biblical standard for both leaders and members. Protect the flock from error.

3. Build the church on spiritual maturity and practical ministry—especially when it comes to making disciples, church discipline, generosity, and stewardship. Decide from the onset to give a good portion of the church income to outreach and mission work. The more that a church gives, the more God blesses. Develop strong leaders who love the Lord.

4. Church planting will thrive on good worship, heartfelt prayers, and honest testimony about what God is doing. If a church is going to be alive, it must have good worship services that encourage the hearts of the people and must be free of conflict, open to all people, joyful, and exuberant. Nothing hurts a ministry more than conflict and lifelessness.

5. Saturate the community with the Gospel. A church's presence must be felt in their territory so that no living soul in that community is without a witness for Jesus. Everyone needs the opportunity to say "yes" or "no" to a Gospel invitation. Be willing to work with other Bible-believing churches so that they too can witness the awakening. Build the kingdom of heaven on earth.

6. The greatest advantage of new churches is that the decision-making process is quicker and new churches are much more prone to be proactive and much less indecisive (they actually do something!). Guard the decision-making process so that it is a well-oiled machine and does not get clogged-up with pettiness, unbelief, and inhibition.

7. There must be a move of God in the church before there can be a move of God in the community. The work and the power of the Holy Spirit are needed so that he is unhindered by the ways of man. Doing the church man's way is always disastrous and predictable. Doing church God's way multiplies believers and ministries to greatly impact a region.

8. The greatest church planter in the history of the church was the apostle Paul. The manual for church planting is the book of Acts. Read it and use it to model the church. When Christian leaders read the history of the early church, they note how big doctrine (*doctrine* refers to *teaching*) was and how hard the apostles fought against error.

9. The essential Gospel doctrine is the issue of salvation. Regeneration comes by the Holy Spirit. People repent of their sins, and they are sanctified by the Word. He will separate them from the world. They are faithful to the church and the Great Commission of Jesus. These are evidences of saving grace. Salvation is not just a decision and a matter of "getting wet"—it is *radical change.*

Chapter 4

The Old Testament Law, History, Wisdom, and Prophets

Open thou my eyes, that I may behold wondrous things out of Thy law. —Psalm 119:18

The Old Testament has four grand divisions: the law, from Genesis to Deuteronomy (five books); the "history books," from Joshua to Esther (twelve books); the poetry passages, from Job to Song of Solomon (five books); and the prophets, from Isaiah to Malachi (seventeen books). They were written over a thousand-year period, from 1400 to 400 BC.

The study of the Old Testament is essential because it is the foundation of all of scripture and has the stories that have endured time. Jesus attested to the fulfillment of the law and the prophets in Matthew 5:17-18. Peter confirmed the significance of all scripture in 1 Peter 1:10-11 and 2 Peter 1:20-21. In 2 Timothy 3:16, Paul said that all scripture is inspired ("God breathed").

The law tells of the beginning of man and affirms God as the Creator of the heavens and the earth. There's the narrative of Noah, Abraham, Isaac, Jacob, and Joseph. It gives the account of Moses and the Ten Commandments,

149

his calling and ministry in the wilderness, the construction of the tabernacle, and the fight against idolatry. The law is the moral code of most governments and cultures.

The historical books cover the days of Joshua crossing over into the Promised Land, the period of the judges and kings, the divided kingdom, the exile to Babylon, the return to repair the walls and rebuild the temple, and the story of Esther in Persia. In the books of Kings, there is no one like David, who slayed Goliath and planned the construction of the temple. He became the standard for all the kings that followed.

In Old Testament poetry, there is the classic on suffering in Job, 150 psalms and the thirty-one chapters of Proverbs, the hard view of life without God in Ecclesiastes, and the eight chapters on marital love in Song of Solomon. These are the writings and compositions of the kings of Israel and their psalmists. Psalm and Proverbs identify with every human emotion and struggle.

Then there are the books of the prophets—seventeen truth-packed books on the history of man's sinfulness and God's graciousness. There are the major prophets Isaiah, Jeremiah, Ezekiel, and Daniel, and the minor prophets, from Hosea to Malachi. They are full of messianic prophecies and pointed judgments. The prophets were men of God who preached the Word despite great odds.

The Old Testament is the backdrop for understanding the New Testament. The true God is the God of the Hebrews because through them came the Messiah, the Savior of the world. They were chosen because they gave the world Jesus. Every writer, with the exception of Luke, came from Abraham's seed. Though the Hebrews rejected the God of the Bible, who became flesh, his truth still stands.

1. The Old Testament reveals the God who created the heavens and the earth.

2. The Old Testament tells the great stories of the men and women of faith.

3. The Old Testament gives an exalted and awesome picture of the true God.

4. The Old Testament tells of the promised Messiah, who is Savior and Lord.

5. The Old Testament warns of judgment, offers mercy, and shows love.

Chapter 5
The New Testament Gospels

And I saw another angel fly in the midst of heaven, having the everlasting gospel to preach unto them that dwell on the earth, and to every nation, and kindred, and tongue, and people... —Revelation 14:6

(Note: See Ministry Helps 1–6, from "Forty-Two Parables of Jesus" to "Seven Last Words of Jesus on the Cross," for the figures named in this lesson.)

The Gospel writers all wrote twenty to thirty years after the death and resurrection of Jesus (with the exception of John, who wrote fifty to sixty years after the Lord's death and resurrection). Matthew targeted the Jews, Mark the Romans, Luke the Greeks, and John, the Jews and Gentiles.

Matthew was known as Levi the tax collector. He was one of the eleven apostles. Mark was a missionary with Paul and Barnabas. Luke was a Gentile physician who was a companion of Paul. John was an apostle and leader of the early church. He had been a fisherman before his call to be a "fisher of men."

Matthew gives the account of the temptation of Jesus in the wilderness, the Sermon on the Mount, the Olivet Discourse, and the Great Commission. Mark is the Gospel of action with the word immediately sprinkled throughout the text. There is an emphasis on prayer and miracles.

Luke has the most detail on the birth of Jesus and includes stories like the Good Samaritan, the prodigal son, the rich man in hellfire, and Zacchaeus's conversion. John gives heaven's view of the birth of Jesus, utilizes "I am" statements to identify Jesus as God, and teaches about the Holy Spirit.

The Gospels have at least forty-two parables, two of which are found only in John 10 (the Door and the Good Shepherd). At least fifty-seven titles are used for the Lord Jesus in the New Testament. Some thirty-four miracles are recorded. The Lord fulfilled more than forty prophecies of the Old Testament.

Jesus was in constant altercations with the scribes, Pharisees, lawyers, and Sadducees. They challenged him for healing on the Sabbath. They accused him of being demon possessed. They asked him difficult questions. They could not hide their hatred for him. They plotted his death for many years.

On the night of his betrayal (the disciples all scattered), there were six trials before Jewish and Roman authorities. He was mocked, beaten, spit upon, crowned with thorns, stripped, and, finally, crucified. He spoke the seven last words (or statements) from the cross, where the sun "went out" and it was dark for three hours.

The Gospel is his death, burial, and resurrection. That is what the apostles preached. The Gospels tell the narrative of the Lord's life. It is not the total story as John 21:25 notes, but it is the perfect story because God inspired those who wrote the words of the New Testament. They tell the greatest story ever told!

Chapter 6

The Acts of the Holy Spirit

Then Peter said unto them, Repent, and be baptized every one of you in the name of Jesus Christ for the remission of sins, and ye shall receive the gift of the Holy Ghost. —Acts 2:38

This book is the Bible's story of the birth of the church. It is called 'The Acts of the Apostles," but the title "The Acts of the Holy Spirit" is more appropriate because the book of Acts records what happened when the Spirit of God filled the souls of the Jews and Gentiles. There is no church and no Gospel without the baptism and filling of the Holy Spirit.

There is much division on the work of the Holy Spirit; but for the purpose of this teaching, there is one baptism of the Spirit, and it is at the point of true salvation (Romans 8:9; 1 John 3:24; 4:13). And yet there are repeated fillings in the life of every believer (Ephesians 5:18). The reference in Ephesians is better understood as "keep being filled with and controlled by the Spirit."

The mighty acts of the Holy Spirit are witnessed at Pentecost, when three thousand men were saved from the nations that gathered in Jerusalem under the preaching of Peter. Five thousand more were saved when Peter and John healed a lame man, and then Peter preached again. These figures do not reflect the families of these men, who were added to the church as well.

Many estimate that at least twenty thousand had been saved after these two events. Acts records the persecution of the apostles who kept praying and speaking in the boldness of the Holy Spirit, the sins of Ananias and Sapphira who lied to the Spirit, and calling of the seven men who were appointed to serve the church whose qualification was to be filled with the Holy Spirit of God.

Stephen was full of the Holy Spirit when he preached and was martyred. Led by the Spirit, Philip preached Jesus and baptized the Ethiopian eunuch.

Ananias restored Saul of Tarsus's sight and prayed that he be filled with the Holy Spirit.

When Peter preached in Cornelius's house, the Spirit of God fell upon the people.

The Holy Spirit separated Paul and Barnabas as apostles. Paul introduced the Spirit of God to the disciples at Ephesus. Later on, he encouraged the Ephesian elders, whom the Spirit had made overseers of the flock of God. The work of the Holy Spirit is evident throughout the twenty-eight chapters of Acts.

There were times when new believers spoke in tongues as they were filled with the Holy Spirit, and there were times when they did not. The Spirit worked to save Jews and Gentiles alike, but as the pages turn, more Gentiles responded to the Gospel message than did Jews while the church multiplied.

Chapter 7

The New Testament Epistles

And account that the long-suffering of our Lord is salvation; even as our beloved brother Paul also according to the wisdom given unto him hath written unto you; As also in all his epistles, speak- ing in them of these things; in which are some things hard to be understood, which they that are unlearned and un- stable wrest, as they do also the other scriptures, unto their own destruction.
—2 Peter 3:15–16

The epistles are the letters of the apostles to the churches of the first-generation Christians. Thirteen are identified as written by Paul, one by James, two by Peter, three by John, one by Jude, and one unknown— but all inspired by the Holy Spirit—for a total of twenty- one letters. The New Testament is comprised of these epistles plus the four Gospels and the books of Acts and Revelation.

The epistles deal with truth and error. They describe the model church and explain the need for discipline to maintain order and holiness. They reveal how the Lord set the church up with a team of elders who rule and a team of deacons who serve. The apostolic letters tell about the true nature of salvation, gifts of the Spirit, spiritual warfare, perseverance in suffering, and the sure marks of a believer, to name only a few of the themes.

The pastoral epistles were written to two young pastors, Timothy and Titus. The general epistles were written to a particular church and applied to the church as a whole. Both doctrine (the teaching of the apostles) and practical living are found in these inspired letters. The closer a church abides by what is written there, the more the blessings of heaven reside on them. The New Testament church was evangelistic and missionary through and through.

It is difficult to prefer one epistle over another, but the book of Romans has all the resources to build a strong missionary church that enables the reader to fully develop a Christian worldview. Each epistle has something to contribute to the development of the Christian character. Hebrews explains the background of the Old Testament and every promise of God fulfilled in the life and sacrifice of the Lord Jesus. Truly, these epistles inspire the soul.

Paul wrote four of his epistles from behind iron bars: Ephesians, Philippians, Colossians and Philemon. They're called the Prison Epistles. These letters of faith came from men who paid the price for the Gospel as it went out to where it had not been known before. They exalt the Lord Jesus, give glimpses of prophecy, warn people about the last days, teach the importance of prayer, give instructions on family life, and tell about stalwart servants of the early church.

Revelation can be counted among the epistles, but it will be examined separately due to its prophetic nature.

Read the epistles. Teach them to the church so that the Gospel light shines!

Chapter 8
The Revelation of Jesus

The Revelation of Jesus Christ, which God gave unto him, to shew unto his servants things which must shortly come to pass; and he sent and signified it by his angel unto his servant John: Who bare record of the word of God, and of the testimony of Jesus Christ, and of all things that he saw. Blessed is he that readeth, and they that hear the words of this prophecy, and keep those things which are written therein: for the time is at hand. —Revelation 1:1–3

This is one of the most powerful books in the Word of God (and they're all powerful). The church planter and Gospel preacher must have a love for the Bible and a heart to search it out and apply it to life and ministry. This is pure prophecy, but there is much to say about practical living here. Revelation starts with a blessing for those who read and hear the words. It continues

Notes

with colorful language, powerful images of judgment, and warnings to live right.

Here, Christians have the vision of the exalted Christ, and each of the twenty-two chapters adds to that glory and image. There are seven letters to the churches of Asia Minor (present-day Turkey). The Lord Jesus is direct and corrective in his instructions. Two churches are not in any way rebuked while the church of Laodicea was given an especially strong warning. Each church was offered overcoming gifts from the Savior.

The reader is transported from the earth to heaven, sees the throne, and hears the songs of the Lamb. He tastes the true worship present there. Then Revelation begins to unfold a series of twenty-one judgments represented by seals, trumpets, and vials. During these judgments, 144,000

Jewish evangelists are sent to the ends of the earth. The two witnesses appear and prophesy in the holy city.

Two beasts appear on the earth: one is identified as the Anti-Christ and the other as the false prophet. The reader sees Babylon the great harlot and Babylon the city—and their imminent judgment from God. What follows is the marriage supper of the Lamb and Armageddon, when the saints come from on high with the Lord back to the earth. Then there is the millennium kingdom of Christ on earth, the bondage of Satan, and the damnation of the beasts.

The New Jerusalem comes down from heaven. It is a jeweled city where the sons of Israel and the apostles of Christ are named, and all the faithful from the ages are rewarded. Revelation concludes with views of the crystal river flowing from the throne of God and the tree of life bearing twelve fruits.

In the final verses, the reader takes in the warnings from the lips of Jesus to those still serving upon the earth. The last Gospel invitation is found in Revelation 22:17. The final line is "The grace of our Lord Jesus Christ be with you all. Amen" (Revelation 22:21).

Bible Doctrines

*And they were astonished at
his doctrine: for he taught
them as one that had authority, and not as the scribes.
—Mark 1:22*

The word doctrine refers to teaching, belief, and knowledge. Sound doctrine affirms what the Bible teaches as a whole, not just what is in one verse. God is infinite, holy, unchanging, all-powerful, all-knowing, and all-present. God is "other" than what man is. Men must be careful in comparing themselves to God, for he all-wise and none can really compare to Him. His many names in scripture represent his attributes.

Some doctrines are not named but are clear in scripture. For example, the Trinity is a historic Christian doctrine.

It is evident as early as Genesis 1:2, 26; 3:22. Jesus commissioned the church to baptize in the name of the Father, Son, and Holy Ghost. The Trinity is found in Titus 3:4–6. The Lord is God the Father, God the Son, and God the Holy Spirit. The Holy Spirit is not an "it." He is God.

There is the doctrine of scripture. That is the belief in the infallibility, reliability, and inerrancy of the original text. Most do not work in the original languages—Hebrew,

Notes

Aramaic, and Greek—but Christians believe that God, who inspired the men who wrote his Word, can also preserve it.

There is the doctrine of Jesus. He is the Creator (Colossians 1:16-17). He is the Son of God in Daniel 3:25 and the angel of the Lord in Judges 13:21-22. He is God in the flesh and one with the Father according to John 14:9. He is the only Savior of the world (John 14:6, Acts 4:12). Jesus is both the Son of God and God the Son. How can that be? He is God. God can do what we cannot.

There's also the doctrine of angels. They are not glorified men or children in heaven. They are above men now (Psalms 8:5) but will be below them in heaven (1 Corinthians 6:3). God is and forever has been eternal. Then there are created beings: angels, men, and lower forms of life. Angels and men are created eternal. But angels can be holy and also be unholy (like Satan, who is the chief fallen angel).

There is the doctrine of man. He was created for fellowship with God, but man rebelled and disobeyed. Man is now fallen and born with orginal sin. He needs the Savior. Sin affects man's mind, body, and spirit. It has a corrupting influence. However, the Spirit and the Word at work in the heart keeps sin in check. All men sin against God. But by grace through faith in Jesus, men can be saved from sin.

Then there's the doctrine of the Holy Spirit, the church, the Christian life, missions, and prophecy. These doctrines are not taught just in one place in scripture, but they are found by cross referencing the entire text. For example, the missionary teaching of the Bible is found in the call of Abraham and Jonah, the coming of Christ to earth, and in the commissions that are found in every Gospel.

Chapter 10

Church History

Unto him be glory in the church by Christ Jesus- throughout all ages, world without end. Amen.
—Ephesians 3:21

Church history helps us see what historic Christian faith looks like and the price each generation paid to "earnestly contend for the faith which was once delivered unto the saints" (Jude 3). One of the greatest benefits of church history is the study of Christian biographies. That leads to the study of martyrs and heroes of faith. These inspiring stories tell about preachers, missionaries, social reformers, and linguists who made an impact on the nations.

The church was born in Jerusalem and was quickly exported to the known world to wherever Roman roads went. The first generation was led by the apostles, and the subsequent generation was led by those called the church fathers. This was the time when the Bible was established: the New Testament, about 190 AD, and the Old Testament, around 300 AD.

The edict of Milan in 313 AD changed everything. The Christian faith was legitimized by Constantine. Many who were not true believers were swept into the church.

The church became institutionalized, big buildings were built, a hierarchy in church leadership was developed, and the pure Gospel message was lost. The church has not recovered to this day. When churches venerate relics and icons, and revel in pageantry and titles, they miss the Gospel of Jesus.

Mohammed founded Islam and took over the epicenter of the faith. In 638 AD, Jerusalem fell; and by 722 AD, Muslims invaded Europe, conquering Spain and Portugal. In 1095, the Roman Catholic pope first called for crusades against the Muslims. So-called Christian men marched against them and murdered heretical Christians, Muslims, and Slavs.

The mystical age followed the Dark Ages for the established church. It was when men like Francis of Assisi, Italy, became devoted to Christ above the church. The downside of mysticism was that experience was placed on equal footing with the exposition of scripture. That is the error of the charismatics today. Then a fresh wind came blowing through the Church with the rise of the reformers. These men called Europe, the base of the Christian faith, back to the Bible.

Men and women in every age have been found to be faithful, but the church as a whole was apostate. Fortunately there were men like John Wycliffe who returned the church to the scriptures. Martin Luther of Germany spurred a revolution against the beliefs and practices of the church with the message of "justification by faith," which was in direct contrast to the erroneous teaching that works could earn salvation.

John Calvin brought about a more biblical and God-centered perspective for Reformation churches. Great missionary movements and worldwide evangelistic thrusts were born with the return to scripture. God mightily used John Wesley, George Whitefield, and Jonathan Edwards to bring about powerful conversions and awakening and he raised up men like David Brainerd, William Carey, David Livingstone, and Hudson Taylor to open up missionary work.

In the last few generations, there has been dramatic growth of the charismatic movement that claims five hundred million adherents today. Along with an emphasis on the gifts of the Spirit, there is the Prosperity Gospel, a non-biblical and heretical teaching that claims that God is obligated by faith to provide wealth and health. As a result, charlatans have multiplied.

There have been mass evangelism and church growth movements that have neglected discipleship and birthed easy believism. More contemporary trends have produced extreme culturally accommodating churches that get the un-churched into services with entertainment and short messages. This has resulted in a faith that is a mile wide and an inch deep. The authority of the Bible is played down while the culture is played up.

Yet there are biblically aligned churches and ministries around the globe that are witnessing Muslim background believers, Hindus, Buddhist, animists, nominal Christians, and Jews, among many others that are being regenerated and living under the Lordship of Christ.

Chapter 11

Christian Apologetics

But sanctify the Lord in your hearts: and be ready always to give an answer to every man that asketh you a reason of the hope that is in you with meekness and fear...
—1 Peter 3:15

Apologetics is the defense of what Christians believe to be true. (It is not an apology.) The Christian truth can be proven and verified by faith and reason. It centers on the resurrection. There were eyewitnesses, transformed apostles, and many physical evidences that validate this foundation of all Christian belief.

Here are the basic arguments of the faith: The Bible is trustworthy. Jesus was God in the flesh. He proved his identity by overcoming death.

There are more New Testament manuscripts than any other accepted ancient literature. There are also less differences in these manuscripts than other historic literature. There is less time between the date when the New Testament was written and the date of the copies on the manuscripts of other ancient writings.

The Bible's human authors record the good, the bad, and the ugly about the characters of the greatest book

163

ever written and the world's most widely read. The writers of the ancient world attested to the truth of scripture. Archaeology confirms the biblical record. The Dead Sea scrolls affirmed the accuracy of the Bible. The western calendar is based on the birth of Jesus. The belief and practices of Christians can be found in every generation since Jesus's earthly ministry. Jesus was God in the flesh. Miracles are recorded. Ancient documents confirm his existence and his mighty works. Luke is careful to give us historical markers that place the reader in the first century.

Some believe that Jesus did not actually die, but his death had been verified. Roman soldiers were professional executioners. Others say his body was stolen. The disciples were frightened and scattered. They could not get past the guards. The Romans were not suspects—they were paid off by the Jewish leaders to say that the body was stolen. The Jewish leaders did not steal it. They would have produced it, if they could have, to discount his resurrection.

There is the defense of the faith in reference to history. There is also the defense of the faith in matters of culture. Culture chips away at biblical faith.

Many biblical mandates and morals are dismissed as merely cultural and not applicable today. The Christian worldview of the first century ought to be the same Christian worldview for today. There are issues like abortion, homosexuality, and the roles of men and women that usurp the standards of scripture. The truth of God is unchanging and is not subject to the judgments of men.

There are many questions about how life began. Bible-believing Christians affirm that God created the heavens and earth in six days just a few millennia ago—not billions of years ago as evolutionists contend.

The atheist says that there is no god.

The agnostic says that we cannot know God.

But the Christian says that he is, he can be known, and he loves man.

World religions and Christian cults present a challenge.

Religions all seek to reach God by works, but still fall short.

Cults embrace heresy in the name of Jesus.

The world has 1 billion Muslims, 650 million Hindus, 300 million Buddhists, 200 million Chinese religionists, and over 1 billion nominal Christians who have no true devotion to Christ and the Christian lifestyle. All these roads lead to hell. All Christian cults lead to hellfire too, even though many of them deny its existence. As stated before, works and human merit fail to get man to heaven.

The grace of God and faith in Jesus alone prevails. There are thousands of ways that are marked "Heaven." Jesus said, "Enter ye at the strait gate: for wide is the gate, and broad is the way, that leadeth to destruction, and many there be which go in thereat: Because strait is the gate, and narrow is the way, which leadeth unto life, and few there be that find it" (Matthew 7:13–14).

Remember that there is only one Savior and one way to heaven!

Chapter 12
Spiritual Warfare

For though we walk in the flesh, we do not war after the flesh: (For the weapons of our warfare are not car- nal, but mighty through God to the pulling down of strong holds)... —2 Corinthians 10:3-4

Most ministers overlook the spiritual reality of unseen forces. They are not aware that Satan will oppose their work, disrupt their family life, try them with financial pressures, attack their family's health, and send antagonists in the life of the church to oppose biblical leadership and any soul- winning efforts.

Ephesians 6:10-18 is the best-known passage on spiritual warfare. Every man of God needs to know it and understand how it works in his life and in those whom he leads. The admonition there is to "be strong in the Lord, and in the power of his might." That cannot happen without much time in the Word of God and prayer.

The prophet Daniel knew that when he set out to give himself to a three-week fast (Daniel 10:2-3). The angel who came to him said, "O man greatly beloved, fear not: peace be unto thee, be strong, yea, be strong" (Daniel 10:19). Spiritual battle makes believers weak at first, but

165

they can be strong with the touch of God!

Believers quickly see how inadequate they are when they deal with spiritual battle, but they also know the power of God when he gives them what they need to fight for souls. When Elisha's servant was fearful, the prophet asked the Lord to open his eyes to see "they that be with us are more than they that be with them" (2 Kings 6:15-17).

The apostle John spoke similar words in 1 John 4:4: "Greater is he that is in you, than he that is in the world." The work of the wicked one is just as John 10:10 says, "To steal, and to kill, and to destroy." He can oppress believers, but not possess them. Only the Holy Spirit can possess a true believer.

James 4:7 says to resist the devil. First Peter 5:8-9 also exhorts us to resist the enemy of our soul. In both passages, it is fitting to note that there is a call to humility. What can trip up a man of God more than any other issue? It is spiritual pride and an exalted sense of self. Christians are called to the cross on earth, not the crown! Matthew 16:24 affirms that.

Another part of spiritual battle is dealing with opposition in the life of the church. Paul wrote in 2 Timothy 3:5, "Having a form of godliness, but denying the power thereof..." In Titus 1:16, he says, "They profess that they know God; but in works they deny him..." Not everyone who says that they are the Lord's is working for him.

How did the old warrior handle those who opposed the faith and the progress of the Gospel ministry?

> *And the servant of the Lord must not strive; but be gentle unto all men, apt to teach, patient, In meekness instructing those that oppose themselves; if God peradventure will give them repentance to the acknowledging of the truth; And that they may recover themselves out of the snare of the devil, who are taken captive by him at his will. (2 Timothy 2:24-26)*

Paul did not want men of God to fight in the church but fight on their knees. He wanted them to teach the truth and seek to win over the very men who opposed them. Life is a relentless spiritual battle. What are the stakes? The glory of God and the souls of men!

Part VII

The Great Missionary of the New Testament

By whom we have received grace and apostleship, for obedience to the faith among all nations, for his name...But now is made manifest, and by the scriptures of the prophets, according to the commandment of the ever-lasting God, made known to all nations for the obedience of faith...
—Romans 1:5, 16:26

Paul, the apostle to the Gentiles, is believed to have started at least twenty churches on two continents. He had three missionary journeys that each covered three, four, and five years. Most of the churches he planted were watered with his sweat and blood—literally. He wrote thirteen letters to those churches, and some Bible teachers add Hebrews to that legacy.

The apostle preached and ministered in all kinds of situations, locations and circumstances, including the marketplaces of Athens and the sacred places of Jerusalem. He witnessed out on the streets, in prisons, on ships, and in synagogues. Wherever he went, people were saved and churches were established. He was a man that was hated on earth but loved in heaven. Very few churches today would tolerate his zeal for souls.

A close reading of the New Testament will reveal a man who was fearless, sacrificial, and incredibly tough, but those traits were coupled with a tender heart for the perishing. His experience on the road to Damascus forever changed him from being the Christians' manic chief persecutor to becoming the church's most compelling preacher. He held the Gospel light high, and he lived the Gospel out right.

So what about Paul's life is so extraordinary and encouraging for today? The following answers the question:

1. He preached Jesus had risen (Acts 9:20; 1 Corinthians 2:2, 15:3-4).

2. He was bold and courageous (Acts 9:27, 29).

3. He had power with God and man (Acts 14:3).

4. He suffered (Acts 14:19-20, 2 Cor. 11:23-28). But he kept going!

5. He saw salvation and awakening wherever he went (Acts 16:25-34).

6. He worked for Satan's defeat and Christ's honor (Acts 19:17-20).

7. He had mighty men of faith who joined him (Acts 20:4).

8. He lived simply and humbly (Acts 20:33-35).

9. He served with a clear conscience and called men up (Acts 24:16, 25).

10. He appealed to the lowest and the highest (Acts 26:28-29, 27:23-25).

It has also been said that the apostle Paul had such zeal that when he came to town, he started a revival or a riot.

The narrative of the Acts of the Holy Spirit will bear that out. He was utterly devoted to the Lord Jesus. He paid whatever price that was required of him to get the Gospel out to those who needed it most. He threw the door wide open to heaven and urged men in!

Notes

169

Part VIII

Ministry Helps

Chapter 1

Forty-Two Parables of Jesus

- Lamp on stand – Matthew 5:14-15; Mark 4:21-22; Luke 8:16,11:33

- Wise and foolish builders – Matthew 7:24-27, Luke 6:47-49

- New cloth on old garment – Matthew 9:16, Mark 2:21, Luke 5:36

- New wine in old bottles – Matthew 9:17, Mark 2:22, Luke 5:37-38

- Four soils – Matthew 13:3-8,18-23; Mark 4:3-8, 14-20; Luke 8:5-8,11-15

- Tares among the wheat – Matthew 13:24-30, 36-43

- Mustard seed – Matthew 13:31-32, Mark 4:30-32, Luke 13:18-19

- Yeast in the meal – Matthew 13:33, Luke 13:20-21

- Hidden treasure – Matthew 13:44

- Pearl of great price – Matthew 13:45-46

- Fishing net – Matthew 13:47-50

- Household treasures – Matthew 13:52

- Lost sheep – Matthew 18:12-14, Luke 15:4-7

- Unmerciful servant – Matthew 18:23-34

- Workers in the vineyard – Matthew 20:1-16

- Obedient son and disobedient son – Matthew 21:28-32

- Wicked workers – Matthew 21:33-44, Mark 12:1-11, Luke 20:9-18

- Invitation to wedding dinner – Matthew 22:2-14

- Signs of the fig tree – Matthew 24:32-35, Mark 13:28-29, Luke 21:29-31

- Wise and foolish virgins – Matthew 25:1-13

- Three servants and talents – Matthew 25:14-30

- Sheep and goats separated – Matthew 25:31-46

- Growing seed – Mark 4:26-29

- Be watchful servants – Mark 13:35-37, Luke 12:35-40

- Moneylender forgives debts – Luke 7:41-43

- Good Samaritan – Luke 10:30-37

- Friend in need – Luke 11:5-8

- Rich man builds bigger barns – Luke 12:16-21

- Wise and foolish servants – Luke 12:42-48, Matthew 24:45-51

- Unfruitful fig tree – Luke 13:6-9

- Lowest seat at the feast – Luke 14:7-14

Notes

173

- Invitation to a great supper – Luke 14:16–24

- Building a tower and a king going to war – Luke 14:28–33

- Lost coin – Luke 15:8–10

- Prodigal son – Luke 15:11–32

- Unjust steward – Luke 16:1–8

- Rich man and Lazarus – Luke 16:19–31

- Master and his servant – Luke 17:7–10

- Widow and the judge – Luke 18:2–8

- Pharisee and publican – Luke 18:10–14

- Ten servants and the ten pounds – Luke 19:12–27

- Sheep, gate, and shepherds – John 10:1–5, 7–18

Chapter 2

Fifty-Seven Titles for the Lord Jesus

(Scholars have actually identified two hundred titles in the Bible.)

- Emmanuel – Matthew 1:23

- King of the Jews – Matthew 2:2

- Governor – Matthew 2:6

- Jesus of Nazareth the Nazarene – Matthew 2:23

- Christ – Matthew 16:20

- Master – Matthew 23:8, 10

- Son of Man – Mark 10:33

- Dayspring – Luke 1:78

- Consolation of Israel – Luke 2:25

- Prophet – Luke 24:19

- Word of God – John 1:1

Notes

- Lamb of God – John 1:29

- Son of God – John 1:34

- The King of Israel – John 1:49

- Messiah – John 4:25-26

- Bread of Life – John 6:35

- Light of the World – John 8:12

- Good Shepherd – John 10:11-14

- Resurrection and Life – John 11:25

- The Way, the Truth, the Life – John 14:6

- True Vine – John 15:1

- God – John 20:28

- Lord – Acts 2:25

- Righteous One – Acts 3:14

- Prince of Life – Acts 3:15

- The Just One – Acts 7:52

- Deliverer – Romans 11:26

- The Rock – 1 Corinthians 10:4

- Head of the Church – Ephesians 1:22-23

- Creator – Colossians 1:16

- Mediator – 1 Timothy 2:5

- The Righteous Judge – 2 Timothy 4:8

- The Captain of Salvation – Hebrews 2:10

- Apostle – Hebrews 3:1

- High Priest – Hebrews 3:1

- The King of Righteousness – Hebrews 7:2

- The King of Peace – Hebrews 7:2

- Author and Finisher of Faith – Hebrews 12:2

- Great Shepherd – Hebrews 13:20

- Chief Cornerstone – 1 Peter 2:6

- Bishop of Souls – 1 Peter 2:25

- Chief Shepherd – 1 Peter 5:4

- Word of Life – 1 John 1:1

- Advocate – 1 John 2:1

- Savior of the World – 1 John 4:14

- Faithful Witness – Revelation 1:5

- First Begotten of the Dead – Revelation 1:5

- Prince of the Kings of the Earth – Revelation 1:5

- Alpha and Omega – Revelation 1:8

- Almighty – Revelation 1:8

- The Amen – Revelation 3:14

- Lion of Judah – Revelation 5:5

- Bridegroom – Revelation 19:7

- The Faithful and True – Revelation 19:11

- King of Kings and Lord of Lords – Revelation 19:16

- Root and Offspring of David – Revelation 22:16

- Bright and Morning Star – Revelation 22:16

Notes

Chapter 3

Thirty-Four Miracles of Jesus

- Healing of the centurion's servant – Matthew 8:5–13

- He calms the stormy sea – Matthew 8:23–27

- Cure of the two demon possessed men – Matthew 8:28–34

- Healing of the paralytic – Matthew 9:1–8

- Raises Jairus's daughter from the dead – Matthew 9:18–26

- Opens the eyes of two blind men – Matthew 9:27–31

- He heals the mute man – Matthew 9:32–33

- Restores man with withered hand – Matthew 12:9–14

- Frees a blind and dumb man from a demon – Matthew 12:22

- Feeds five thousand men – Matthew 14:13–21

- Heals a Canaanite woman's daughter of a demon – Matthew 15:21–28

- Feeds four thousand men – Matthew 15:32–39

- Delivers a boy from a demon – Matthew 17:14–21

- Opens the eyes of two blind men – Matthew 20:29–34

- Withers the fig tree – Matthew 21:18-22

- Frees man of an unclean spirit in a synagogue Mark 1:21-28

- Cures Peter's mother-in-law – Mark 1:29-34

- Heals a leper – Mark 1:40-45

- Cures a deaf and mute man – Mark 7:31-37

- Opens the eyes of a blind man – Mark 8:22-26

- Catches great number of fish – Luke 5:1-11

- Raises widow of Nain's son from the dead – Luke 7:11-17

- Cures woman with issue of blood – Luke 8:43-48

- Heals woman of spirit of infirmity, bent over for eighteen years Luke 13:10-17

- Cures a man of dropsy on the Sabbath – Luke 14:1-6

- Ten lepers healed – Luke 17:11-19

- Restores the cut off ear of the high priest's servant– Luke 22:50-51

- He rose from the dead! – Luke 24:5-6

- Changes water into wine – John 2:1-11

- Cures nobleman's son – John 4:46-54

- Heals the invalid at the Pool of Bethesda – John 5:1-18

- Opens the eyes of the man born blind – John 9:1-41

- Raises Lazarus from the dead – John 11:1-46

- Catches great number of fishes – John 21:1-14

Notes

179

Chapter 4

Forty Old Testament Prophecies Jesus Fulfilled

Think not that I am come to destroy the law, or the prophets: I am not come to destroy, but to fulfill. —Matthew 5:17

- He would bruise Satan's head – Genesis 3:15, Romans 16:20

- His Star shall rise in Jacob – Numbers 24:17, Matthew 2:2

- His scepter will be in Israel – Numbers 24:17, Matthew 2:2

- He will be the Prophet – Deuteronomy 18:18, Matthew 21:11

- He would break the power of death – Psalm 16:8–11, Acts 2:31–33

- He cried out about being forsaken – Psalm 22:1, Matthew 27:46

- They mocked him – Psalm 22:6–8, Matthew 27:27–31

- His heart was broken – Psalm 22:14, John 19:34

- Hands and feet were pierced – Psalm 22:16, John 19:37

- Lots cast over his garment – Psalm 22:18, John 19:23–24

- He committed himself to God at death – Psalm 31:5, Luke 23:46
- His bones were not broken – Psalm 34:20, John 19:33

- Betrayed by a friend – Psalm 41:9, Matthew 26:14-16

- Jesus would ascend into the heavens – Psalm 68:18, Acts 1:9-11

- Hated without a cause – Psalm 69:4, John 15:25

- Zeal will mark his ministry – Psalm 69:9, John 2:13-17

- He thirst – Psalm 69:21, John19:28

- Gall and vinegar given for his thirst – Psalm 69:21, John 19:28-30

- He will be a stone of offense to the Jews – Psalm 118:22, 1 Peter 2:6-8

- Born of a virgin – Isaiah 7:14, Matthew 1:23

- Jesus is called Emmanuel – Isaiah 7:14, Matthew 1:23

- His ministry will be in Galilee – Isaiah 9:1-2, Matthew 4:12-17

- The Spirit of the Lord will be upon him – Isaiah 11:1-5, Matthew 3:16-17

- He will have a forerunner before him – Isaiah 40:3-5, John 1:19-28

- Jesus is a light to the Gentiles – Isaiah 49:6, 60:3; Acts 13:47-48

- Rejected by his own – Isaiah 53:3, Mark 15:29-32

- Wounded, bruised, chastised, and beaten – Isaiah 53:4-5, Matthew 27:26

- Silent before his accusers – Isaiah 53:7, Matthew 27:11-14

- Buried in a rich man's tomb – Isaiah 53:9, Matthew 27:57-60

Notes

- Crucified among thieves - Isaiah 53:12, Luke 23:33

- Prayed for his persecutors - Isaiah 53:12, Luke 23:34

- Son of David - Jeremiah 23:5, Matthew 1:1-17

- Herod slays Bethlehem children - Jeremiah 31:15, Matthew 2:16-18

- Born in Bethlehem - Micah 5:2; Luke 2:4,11

- Entered Jerusalem on a donkey - Zechariah 9:9, Matthew 21:1-11

- Sold for thirty pieces of silver - Zechariah 11:12, Matthew 26:15

- Money cast in the house of the Lord - Zechariah 11:13, Matthew 27:3-10

- Purchased field with blood money - Zechariah 11:13, Matthew 27:7

- His side was pierced - Zechariah 12:10, John 19:34

- Forsaken by the disciples - Zechariah 13:7, Mark 14:50

Chapter 5

The Six Trials of Jesus

There were six illegal trials held in rapid succession for the Savior of the world. For the man who never sinned, the real sinners were bloodthirsty to see him die. The Jewish trials all declared him guilty, and the Roman trials all declared his innocence. Remarkable! Yet he went to Calvary to bear the punishment of sin. One day it is he who will judge all mankind; it is then when every soul must stand before him.

- First Jewish trial before Annas – John 18:12–14

- Second Jewish trial before Caiaphas – Matthew 26:57–68, John 18:19–24

- Third Jewish trial before Sanhedrin – Luke 22:66–71

- First Roman trial before Pilate – Luke 23:1–5, John 18:28–32

- Second Roman trial before Herod – Luke 23:6–12

- Third Roman trial before Pilate – Luke 23:13–25, John 18:33–19:16

Notes

Chapter 6

Seven Last Words of Jesus on the Cross

These are the Savior's last words at Calvary as his hands and feet were pierced with nails, his brow crowned with thorns, his garments cruelly torn from his body—the spittle of mockers running down his face and the skin flayed from his back and torso from the severe beating. Here was the Lamb of God that takes away the sins of the world (John 1:29)!

This is the pulpit from which he spoke:

- "Father, forgive them; for they know not what they do." (Luke 23:34)

- "Verily I say unto thee, Today shalt thou be with me in paradise." (Luke 23:43)

- "Woman, behold thy son!...Behold thy mother!" (John 19:26–27)

- "Eli, Eli, lama sabachthani" [My God, my God, why hast thou forsaken me?] (Matt. 27:46, Mark 15:34)

- "I thirst." (John 19:28)

- "It is finished." (John 19:30)

- "Father, into thy hands I commend my spirit." (Luke 23:46)

Chapter 7

A Clear Presentation of the Gospel Message

1. Establish a rapport and relationship with them, and believe it or not, this can be done in just a few moments. One way to approach this is with the acronym FIRE. Do not take the same approach with every person. This little tool may be a help in identifying ways to communicate.

   F – Family and friends. Ask them about their family and friends. Be careful not to spend too much time on this so that the opportunity to share the saving grace of Jesus is forfeited.

   I – Interests. Build some common ground by speaking about interests they have. Seek to avoid controversy and distractions that are not relative to the heart of the Gospel. Do not argue about churches or politics.

   R – Religion and background in faith. Discover their worldview and how they see God (without being contentious). Point them to the work of Christ. Find out how they see the Word of God.

   E – Evangelize. Share the basic Gospel message.

185

Have they surrendered their will and given up their sin in order to be saved and live for God? Are they victorious over temptation and sin?

2. Be sure they understand sin and how it separates them from God. Tell them that the penalty of sin is death and that Christ laid down his life for sinners. Explain that he is the only Lord and Savior because he forgives sin and conquered death (Romans 3:23-26, Titus 2:11-14).

3. Men everywhere must repent of their sins and ask for mercy, grace and forgiveness from the Lord. Sin is rebellion against God, dishonor of his person and name, a violation of his law, and rejection of his grace. Repentance is to break off sin and live for the Savior (Romans 3:10-20).

4. It takes faith in Christ alone to save men from their sins (Acts 4:12, Hebrews 11:1, 6). Faith is what pleases God. When it is present, it makes a man faithful and true. When it is absent, there is doubt and discouragement. Faith enables men to see the unseen and to live for eternity and not time.

5. When there is repentance from sin and faith in Christ alone, that person is forever changed. They become a new creature with a hunger and thirst for righteousness (2 Corinthians 5:17, Romans 8:9-11). They are filled with the Spirit of God. God becomes the foremost priority in their lives.

6. The call of the Gospel is in Matthew 16:24: "If any man will come after me, let him deny himself, and take up his cross, and follow me." (Matthew 16:24-27, Ephesians 2:8-10, Romans 10:9-11, 13.) True salvation does not allow a person to live a sinful lifestyle (1 John 2:15-17, 3:5-10).

Chapter 8

Growing in Christian Maturity

Growth is a natural part of life. When a baby is born, he grows. When there is spiritual life, there is likewise growth and development. The teaching that believers can be "baby Christians" all their lives is not so. It comes from a misinterpretation of 1 John 2:12-14.

There are stages of spiritual maturity and degrees of obedience, but growth happens supernaturally just as it does naturally. Consider Ephesians 4:14-16, 1 Peter 2:2-3, and 2 Peter 3:18. There is growth wherever there is life. If there is no apparent growth, there may not be spiritual life.

1. Be sanctified by the Word of God (John 17:17). If there is no hunger for the scripture, regeneration is in question. The Bible is not optional for a new believer. It is the source of the salvation message and the means of training in righteousness (James 1:21, 2 Timothy 3:14-17).

2. Pray with heart and soul. It is by prayer that Christians learn the intercession of the Spirit and line themselves up with the will of God (Romans 8:26-27). Prayer keeps the heart tender and the will submissive. It is by prayer that repentance and confession stay up to date (James 5:16, 1 John 1:9).

Notes

3. Meet often with other believers as the church (Heb.10:23-25, 1 John 2:19). Fellowship brings encouragement and accountability—that is, if it is a Bible-honoring and God-exalting ministry. If it is a fighting church with ungodly leaders, find another place of worship and service (Ephesians 5:3-11).

4. Serve the Lord in the context of the church (Romans 12:1-21). True believers are saved by grace and show their gratitude with good works (Ephesians 2:8-10, Titus 3:1, 8, 14). Good works are the fruit of the Christian life (Matthew 3:8, 10; 12:33-37). If there is no service, there is no salvation.

5. Walk in Christian character (Galatians 5:22-25). There is the fruit of service, but there is also the fruit of a righteous life (2 Peter 1:3-11). If there is a lack of humility, patience, and love (the chief Christian virtues), then there is no maturity. The light of Jesus shines through fit lamps (Luke 12:35).

6. Do the Great Commission of Jesus (Matthew 28:18-20). This is the highest level of spiritual maturity. Any church leader who is unwilling to do the Great Commission should not be appointed because he is disobedient to the mandate for the church (Acts1:8). Take the Gospel out locally and globally. It is his command!

Chapter 9

Principles of Biblical Counseling

What's essential for biblical counseling is knowing the Word of God. In generations past, the man of God was the primary counselor before the advent of secular psychology. Even today, a great number of people go to ministers for counsel and personal guidance. Pastors can only heal the soul with biblical truth.

There are at least two approaches to counseling: the classical approach, which involves listening to uncover issues and follow up with advice. Second, biblical counseling seeks to get to the root of any trouble and get victory over sinful habits and mind-sets. The basis of biblical counseling is finding answers and insights in scripture.

1. Discover where they are in their commitment to Christ. Do they proclaim him—without reservation—as their Lord and Savior? Do they spend time daily applying the Word of God and walking by faith? Are they people of prayer? (Psalms 42:1-2; 63:1-8; 139:1-18, 23-24)

2. If they are not believers, seek to lead them to faith in Christ. This will resolve many issues and give them power to overcome any other point of conflict. A Christian's life is not free from trouble, but problems

can be put into perspective, and resolutions can be found with the Lord's help (Rom. 8:37, 1 John 5:4).

3. Find out why they are hurting or struggling. It may be in their relationships, marriage, struggles in parenting, discernment of the will of God, employment needs, or grief. Hear them out, give them Bible references that apply to their needs, and pray with them by pouring out your heart (Matthew 11:28-30, Heb. 4:11-16).

4. If there is a problem with immorality or unethical behavior, lead them to the place of confession where they agree with God that it is sin. If it is a public sin, they should make public confession. If it is private, they should make amends and reconcile with those affected (James 5:16, 1 John 1:6-9).

5. Men should be cautious about counseling young ladies and women in private. Discretion is crucial, and the subject matter must not become inappropriate or unseemly. It is best for ladies to go to ladies, if at all possible (1 Corinthians 6:18-20, 1 Thessalonians 4:2-8).

6. Be careful with children. It may be best for ladies who know the Word of God to do the counseling for little ones and younger teens. Ladies are better as they are natural nurturers and encouragers. If there are behavioral problems, discover what measures of discipline have been taken and/or have to be recommended (Matthew 18:6, Proverbs 29:15, 17).

Chapter 10

Steps in Church Discipline

The definitive verses for church discipline are Matthew 18:15-20, which ends with the verse that is universally applied to prayer rather than church discipline. How can so many take scripture out of context? The reality is that church discipline is seldom done, and only few churches would tolerate it. In fact, the man of God who dares to do it may become the object of church action.

The passage in Matthew is not the only reference to church discipline. It is clear in the New Testament that church discipline was practiced—1 Corinthians 5, 2 Thessalonians 3:6-15, 3 John 1:9-11, and Revelation 2-3. When a church refuses disciplinary measures, they lose their testimony. (The word church means "the called-out ones," so we are to be a sanctified people.)

1. If a brother or sister sins against another, let the one who was sinned against go to the offender and make things right. If the offender hears and makes amends, the matter is resolved (Matthew 18:15).

   a. Often what is seen as sin for one is not seen as sin for another. There really are times that an offender never intended to hurt the other. Humility on both sides—for the offender to

191

own up to his sin and for the offended to accept repentance— will mend the rift.

b. The call here is to go to the offender and make things right. It is ungodly and a breach of scripture not to do so. It is wrong to speak against the offender without speaking with them first—which is too often the case.

2. If the offender will not hear, take one or two people with you and go to him or her a second time so that there are witnesses of the break in fellowship (Matthew 18:16).

a. This is the step-by-step plan of Jesus to reconcile brothers and sisters in the faith. Taking witnesses enables the offender to see the gravity of the sin and gives the witnesses opportunity to add their voices to the appeal to repent.

b. Galatians 6:1 is another good text to keep close to the heart. It reveals the humility that is needed to bring people back into the right fellowship. Broken relationships with people indicate a broken relationship with God.

3. If the offender will not hear the second plea established by two or three witnesses, then take it to the church. If he or she ignores the church, then they are to be treated as an unbeliever and have no place in the fellowship.

a. Church discipline holds people accountable for their beliefs and actions. It puts the fear of God in them if they have any reverence for the church. Failure to initiate discipline opens the church to all kinds of ungodliness.

b. Strife, backbiting, maliciousness, and slander will no longer be respectable sins. The people of God are "safe" in the place of worship and service. The witness of the church and standards of righteousness are upheld.

Chapter 11

Serving the Lord with Excellence

Not slothful in business; fervent in spirit; serving the Lord...(Romans 12:11)

I press toward the mark for the prize of the high calling of God in Christ Jesus. (Philemon 3:14)

And whatsoever ye do in word or deed, do all in the name of the Lord Jesus, giving thanks to God and the Father by him. (Colossians 3:17)

And whatsoever ye do, do it heartily, as to the Lord, and not unto men; Knowing that of the Lord ye shall receive the reward of the inheritance; for ye serve the Lord Christ. (Colossians 3:23–24)

Notes

Proverbs has ample warnings about the slothful man.

> *He also that is slothful in his work is brother to him*
> *that is a great waster.(Proverbs 18:9)*

Another paints the picture vividly:

> *I went by the field of the slothful, and by the vineyard of the man void of*
> *understanding; And, lo, it was all grown over with thorns, and nettles had*
> *covered the face thereof, and the stone wall thereof was broken down.*
> *(Proverbs 24:30-31)*

1. Be timely, punctual, and "redeeming the time, because the days are evil" (Ephesians 5:16). Work the works of him "while it is day: the night cometh, when no man can work" (John 9:4).

2. The Lord deserves the best, the highest reach, the greatest efforts coupled with our dependence upon him—not sloppy, lax, and shabby work in Christian ministry.

3. Believers should always work harder and give more than what is expected. They should anticipate needs and meet them.

4. They should never call in sick if they are not or take pay they have not earned. Honesty and integrity are basic virtues that spring from true faith.

5. Christian workers reach standards of excellence with a good work ethic and powerful prayer so that they can be fruitful, profitable, and dependable.

6. Christians must never be given to strife, division, slander, whispering, backbiting, manipulation, undermining, and deception. That's the devil's work.

7. Perseverance, a steadfast spirit, resolve, grit, and determination are needed to reach excellence so that obstacles and discouragement do not deter.

8. Work to hear, "Well done, thou good and faithful servant..." (Matthew 25:21).

Chapter 12

Saturation Evangelism

The book of Acts, which records the birth and development of the church, is an incredible story of saturation of the Gospel among the nations. Start in Acts 2:47, which says, "Praising God, and having favour with all the people. And the Lord added to the church daily such as should be saved." Then follow through to Acts 5:14, 42; 6:7; 8:4, 25; 9:31; 11:21; 12:24; 13:49; 16:5; 19:20 as the Word of God multiplied and increased.

1. This is the practical belief that anyone in a territory where there is a local ministry should have the personal opportunity to say "yes" or "no" to a Gospel invitation. That can happen in a number of ways: door-to-door visitation, event evangelism, or service projects in the community.

2. This is not simply a quick few moments of sharing and prayer with people but a time of showing compassion and giving encouragement to souls. One of the greatest ministries that can be done by a local church is to send out prayer teams just to pray for people's needs and take information for further follow-up.

195

3. This would include not only residential outreach but also market and business outreach in getting to know business owners, doing service in schools, and finding ways to improve the community as a means to share the Gospel. Select the kind of people on teams that will represent Christ well.

4. This is a necessary ministry because no one should die without a personal opportunity to repent of and be forgiven for their sins. No one should go out of this world unloved. This is a way to mend the brokenhearted and to listen to, weep with, and ache for the neglected.

5. This is a messy work that can be full of trouble, disappointment, and pain, but that is the nature of working with people and seeing God transform them. So make disciples. Watch souls come out of darkness and walk into light, going from death to life. (People still need the Lord!)

6. This is a great ministry for recovering those who once knew the joys of Christian fellowship. One of Satan's most effective tools is discouragement. There are countless people who have been wounded by the church and by Christian leaders. Man will disappoint, but God never will. We just have to trust him.

7. Grow the church beyond programs by getting to the heart of ministry—rescuing people out of immorality and cultural compromise to live for Christ and become overcomers from their sin. Such a ministry breaks down the barrier between the church and needy souls so that they can come in.

Chapter 13

Home and Hospital Visitation

And daily in the temple, and in every house, they ceased not to teach and preach Jesus Christ. (Acts 5:42)

Therefore they that were scattered abroad went every where preaching the word. (Acts 8:4)

And they, when they had testified and preached the word of the Lord, returned to Jerusalem, and preached the gospel in many villages of the Samaritans. (Acts 8:25)

The historic model for ministry involves visitation, prayer, and meeting practical needs to share the Gospel of Christ. It is never meeting social ills without the Gospel message. Christians are to go and tell, and to do ministry with compassion.

Notes

1. Visit every home or hut, business, school, hospital, nursing home, rehab center, and prison in the region.

2. Utilize tracts, Gospel coins, scripture portions, and Bibles to make Christ known in the community. Be sure that what is given is doctrinally sound.

3. Pray with people wherever you go without being a nuisance. For example, be respectful of hospital regulations and business environments.

    a. Christian workers should use caution and be respectful in places like intensive care units. Work with doctors and the staff, but also give way to them.

    b. Men should not go into ladies' hospital rooms that have closed doors without knocking or having a nurse check first. Make hospital vis- its brief.

4. Men should not go into homes where women are by themselves. It is better to talk in the doorway or outside, if the weather is conducive.

5. Men should not meet with women who are not properly dressed, nor should they walk into an environment where there is drinking, reveling or any ungodly behavior.

6. Adults should not be alone with children or youth in private settings without the expressed consent of parents. It is best not to meet alone.

7. Women should always have a man with them when they visit in a community, unless the ministry targets women only—yet they should not be alone with a man.

8. Be cautious about displays of affection in private like hugs and long embraces. Be discreet in all things. Be wise and edifying in your conversations.

Chapter 14

Pre-Marital Counseling

Every couple who desires a Christian wedding ceremony, intends on a lifetime commitment, and wants their marriage to give glory to God above all, should meet with a man of God for premarital counseling. This is not only done to plan the ceremony but also to examine scripture; share practical steps of merging two families and starting a new one; and examine the faith, family roles, and personalities of the couple.

Here are truths that can be shared in counseling. The recommendation is to have no less than three meetings to pray, share, and work out ceremony details.

Biblical Guidelines

Marriage is built on commitment and not romantic love alone. Commitment works off sacrifice and steadfast devotion while romantic love is often based on feelings and outward appearance.

In marriage, the husband and wife blend their lives together, and they become one. Their children will reflect the strengths and weakness of their sacrificial love for each another.

The strongest verse on marriage is Hebrews 13:4, "Marriage is honourable in all, and the bed undefiled: but whoremongers and adulterers God will judge." Marriage is sacred and holy ground.

Faithfulness to the husband and wife is the foundation of trust and the standard of any true commitment. It is the Bible's mandate for the godly. It is affirmed by a person's deeds and their thought life.

Scriptural Principles

1. The Lord intends for one living man to have one living woman only. Release from marriage comes with death.

2. God hates divorce (Malachi 2:15).

3. Divorce is allowed for adultery and desertion in the case of an unequally yoked marriage (1 Corinthians 7:15), but Christ spoke only on the grounds of adultery or fornication.

4. God's purpose for marriage is to produce godly offspring.

Examination of Ephesians 5:21–33

1. Wives are called to submission unto their husbands (Ephesians 5:22).

2. Husbands have the greater challenge of loving their wives as Christ so loved the church that he gave himself for it (Ephesians 5:25).

3. The husband is the spiritual leader of the family and has the responsibility of one day presenting his wife and children to the Lord (Ephesians 5:27).

4. Husbands are to love their wives as their own bodies (Ephesians 5:28).

5. The scriptures say that a man and woman must leave father and mother and cleave unto his wife or her husband (Ephesians 5:31).

6. Husbands are to love their wives as they love themselves, and wives are to honor and esteem their husbands (Ephesians 5:33).

Questions to Consider:

1. Is your relationship to your partner, first and foremost, a true friendship? Is she or he your closest friend next to Jesus?

2. Do you know each other's strengths and weaknesses? Are you willing to rejoice in the other's strengths and show patience with the weaknesses?

3. What two traits from your parents' marriage do you want to bring to your own?

4. What two flaws from your parents' marriage do you not want to bring into your own?

5. What are four reasons you are getting married?

6. How would you define the husband's and wife's role in the home?

7. What are your convictions on disciplining your children?

8. What three values do you want to be sure you pass on to your children?

9. What five goals do you have in your lifetime? How do you plan to accomplish them?

10. What is your perspective on debt?

11. Do you believe it is important to live on a budget?

12. Do you have dreams and hopes apart from your current vocation?

Notes

How to Be a Godly Wife

The Creator made woman to be the man's helper. That's what the Bible says! Her divine task is to take care of her husband, her home, and her children (Titus 2:3-5). A lady of grace makes the home a place of peace, joy, and security.

This is the will of God expressed for woman. This is why she was created:

1. The wife is the helpmeet (Genesis 2:18).

2. She is a fruitful vine (Psalms 128:3).

3. A godly wife is called to submission (Ephesians 5:22-23, 1 Peter 3:1-2).

4. She is called to diligence in her duties (Proverbs 31:10-31). Her clothing is to be love, wisdom, kindness, strength, dignity, gentleness, peacefulness, compassion, and hospitality.

5. A godly wife is a crown unto her husband (Proverbs 12:4).

How to Be a Godly Husband

God has ordained the husband and father to be the spiritual leader in the home. It is his divine intent for the man to lead the family in devotion to the Word of God, prayer, building up the faith, and to develop a strong worship commitment with like-minded believers. He is also to lead his family in serving the Lord in practical ways through missions and outreach.

When spiritual leadership is neglected, the message of faith is muddled, and Satan then gains easy access to the hearts of family members. Never sacrifice the souls of the family at the altar of the television, and be insistent on having family meals together apart from media and music outlets. Teach the family to follow what's commanded in Deuteronomy 6:5.

The Family Budget

Give the first cut of every check to the Lord through tithes and offerings for the family. If they will honor him, he will honor them (1 Samuel 2:30). The tithe should equal 10 percent of the household gross income.

Pay debts and beware of illegitimate debts (Romans 13:8). An illegitimate debt is when a person owes more on an item that the market value will bring.

Seek to save 10 percent of every paycheck for emergency needs.

Be wise and let the partner in the marriage who has better management skills keep the checkbook. Pray together over major purchases and expenses.

Set aside what is needed to pay for annual taxes.

Practical Ways to Show Love

Get thirty minutes of uninterrupted time together to share your heart with one another.

Write a love letter to your husband or wife-to-be and mail it!

Plan a surprise getaway, day out, or dinner.

Write down the reasons for your love for her or him.

Make every kiss count, and leave no doubt of love and devotion.

Give an unexpected little gift. (It doesn't have to be expensive, but it does need to show that you put some thought into it).

Do something he or she would enjoy even though you might not.

Take a long walk in a place where it can be just the two of you.

Notes

Chapter 15

A Christian Wedding Ceremony

This ceremony can be adapted as needed to include other ministers and family members. The goal is worship. The person of honor is the Lord and then the bride.

Order of Service

Processional of the wedding party

Invocation by the Pastor

Introduction of the ceremony by the Pastor

Giving away of the bride by the father of the bride

Wedding message by the Pastor

Exchange of vows between the bride and the groom

Exchange of rings between the bride and the groom

Lighting of the unity candle by the bride and the groom

Closing remarks by the Pastor

Benediction by the Pastor

Presentation of Mr. and Mrs. Joshua Goforth

Recessional of the wedding party

Wedding Ceremony

Introduction

Let us pray!

Dear friends and family, we are gathered together here in the presence of God and these loved ones for the purpose of marriage. We are witnesses as Joshua and Justine commit themselves to a lifetime of love.

Marriage is the foundation of the home and social order.

In the wisdom of the Almighty, he did not first create the state or the church. He created the home. He gave away the first bride.

We know, from God's perspective, that marriage is a permanent relationship between one man and one woman who are freely and totally committed to each other as companions for life. It is the closest and most tender of all kinships.

"Who gives this woman to this man in marriage?"

Wedding Message

The Christian home is built upon Christ's love.

> Beloved, let us love one another: for love is of God; and every one that loveth is born of God, and knoweth God. He that loveth not knoweth not God; for God is love. In this was manifested the love of God toward us, because that God sent his only begotten Son into the world, that we might live through him. Herein is love, not that we loved God, but that he loved us, and sent his Son to be the propitiation for our sins. Beloved, if God so loved us, we ought also to love one another. (1 John 4:7-11)

Notes

Love never fails.

We have faith, hope, and love— these three—but the greatest of these is love. With such love and devotion, you will half your sorrows and double your joys as man and wife.

> *Submitting yourselves one to another in the fear of the Lord God. Wives, submit yourselves unto your own husbands, as unto the Lord. For the husband is the head of the wife, even as Christ is the head of the church: and he is the saviour of the body. Therefore as the church is subject unto Christ, so let the wives be to their own husbands in every thing. Husbands, love your wives, even as Christ also loved the church, and gave himself for it... (Ephesians 5:21-25)*

We dedicate your home to the Lord, where the Bible will be open and prayers will be common. We commend you to the church as you serve the Lord together, that you might know heaven's full reward. This ceremony reminds us of the marriage to come on high.

> *Let us be glad and rejoice, and give honour to him: for the marriage of the Lamb is come, and his wife hath made herself ready. And to her it was granted that she should be arrayed in fine linen, clean and white: for the fine linen is the righteousness of the saints. And he saith unto me, Write, Blessed are they which are called unto the marriage supper of the Lamb. And he saith unto me, These are the true sayings of God. (Revelation 19:7-9)*

It is our hope that all who witness this wedding will be part of the one to come between Christ and his church.

Wedding Vows

"Joshua, do you take Justine to be your lawfully wedded wife, to have and to hold, to love and to cherish, from this day forward until death do you part? Will you promise to love, honor, and serve her in all things—in sickness and in health, in prosperity and adversity—and to be true and loyal to her and her only as long as you both shall live? Do you?"

"Justine, do you take Joshua to be your lawfully wedded husband, to have and to hold, to love and to cherish, from this day forward until death do you part? Do you promise to love, honor, and serve him in all things—in sickness and in health, in prosperity and adversity—and to be true and loyal to him and him only as long as you both shall live? Do you?"

Exchange of Rings

The ring has been a symbol for all ages as a sacred token of boundless love and unending promises between a man and woman devoted to each other in marriage. It is a circle, without beginning and end.

Before you give the ring to your bride and bridegroom, look at each other's hands. These are the hands of your best friend, young and strong and full of love for you. These are the hands that will work alongside you as you build your future together.

These are the hands that will passionately love you and cherish you through the years and, with the slightest touch, will comfort you like no other. These hands will wipe tears from your eyes—tears of sorrow but mostly tears of joy.

These are the hands that will hold your children. These hands will give you strength when you need it. And these are the hands that will still be reaching for yours—even when they're wrinkled and aged—they'll still be giving you unspoken tenderness with just a touch.

Joshua, do you have the token of your love for Justine?... Place this ring on the ring finger of your wife and repeat after me. Justine, with this ring, I give my love and my loyalty. I give my life and my future in the name of the Father, Son, and Holy Spirit. Amen."

Justine, with the same significance as the ring you just received, the ring you give to your husband is one thing in the world that is least tarnished and most enduring. It speaks to your endless devotion.

Do you possess it as a token of your love for Joshua?... Place the ring on the ring finger of your husband and repeat after me. Joshua, with this ring, I give my love and my loyalty. I give my life and my future in the name of the Father, the Son, and the Holy Spirit. Amen."

Unity Candle

Now that you have pledged your lives together to cherish each other and to serve the Lord as you build a Christian home and family before God and these witnesses, by the virtue of the authority invested in me as a minister of the Gospel, I pronounce you man and wife.

You are no longer two but one in purpose, love, and destiny. May the Lord bless you.

> The Lord bless thee, and
> keep thee: The Lord make his
> face shine upon thee, and be

Notes

gracious unto thee: The Lord lift up his countenance upon thee, and give thee peace. (Num. 6:24-26)

What therefore God hath joined together, let not man put asunder. (Mark 10:9)
Let us pray.
You may kiss the bride!

Presentation

Ladies and gentlemen, I present Mr. and Mrs. Joshua Goforth!

Chapter 16

Baby Dedication

Ezekiel Daniel Montana

Babies are the wonders of creation. Wrapped up in flesh and blood is all the promise of God for this little lad. We only know the first chapter of Ezekiel's life and the rest of the book has yet to be written. Daniel and Kara, along with their parents, will have much to do with what happens in those pages.

We are here to dedicate Ezekiel Daniel to the Lord: his home, future, salvation, mission, protection, and care. The Lord has given him a more-than-wonderful family and a church that loves him, has prayed for him, and will nurture him in the ways of the Lord and in the truth of God's Word.

In the Old and New Testaments, they brought their children to the tabernacle or temple on the eighth day to dedicate them to the Lord with a sacrifice and prayer. Jesus was dedicated in this way. We remember the words of Simeon and Anna as they spoke to the heart of Mary on that sacred day.

Today we follow their example of faith.

Scripture: Matthew 19:13-15

(Pastor selects and prays for the parents and church on their spiritual and moral responsibility to Ezekiel so that he grows to love Jesus.)

Notes

- Parents

    Do you commit your home to the Lord, to the reading of scripture, and your hearts to believing prayer? Do you pledge yourselves to a God-honoring marriage and prayer for your son's salvation and Christian testimony?"

- Church leaders

    Do you offer yourselves as examples in the faith, knowing that this little lad will have his eyes on you and that he will look to you as Christian examples? Will you pledge yourselves to pursue God's highest standards through unceasing prayer and love?

- Church family

    Do you give yourselves to the nurture, love, and affirmation of this lad in the worship and service of the Lord? Will you pray for his guidance, discretion, and purity as a young man? Will you call him by name before the Lord?"

Prayer of Dedication

    Father, we pray for Ezekiel Daniel to grow up in a strong Christian family and in a loving church, where the presence of Jesus is strong. We ask that you save his soul at an early age. Keep him from every evil and harm. Make him like the great heroes of the faith. Let his light shine bright in this dark world!
    (Pastor prays a heartfelt prayer with Ezekiel Daniel in his hands.)

Chapter 17

Funeral

Funeral or memorial services are very personal. Joseph Hart is the brother who crossed over in this service. His wife was Sarah and parents, Joey and Ruth.

Such services are times to tell the truth without hurting the family or being insensitive. Do not preach them into heaven if their testimony was broken and questionable. Do not give false comfort either. It is an opportune time to call people to examine their faith and prepare for their own death, yet leave all judgment in the hands of the Lord.

(If the author knows the person well, he will write a poem to commemorate the life and testimony of the brother or sister. The following poem was written by the author for the man whose home base was in the community where the author served as a senior pastor.)

How Do You Say Goodbye?

Joseph's voice still speaks in our hearts and his presence is known In so many ways, in every day. How we remember life's yesterdays! How do you say "goodbye" to the one you love, the one you've birthed? The brother you took every step with in your youth? How? Oh God, how?

There have been the ticks of golden time that have been a gift from above
These last months, to stop and be still and to cherish a life well lived.
Yet those trying days and treasured moments were too short and too quick
To say all we had to say to the sweetheart, the son, and brother we loved.

In this life, there have been many other "goodbyes:" going off to school,
Moving on to a new place for work, traveling to another part of the globe.
This one is very different though, because, before youth's song was sung,
He's gone and we're left with brokenness and tears and sorrow sore.

Joseph has taken a road none of us have taken before—through death's door.
With vintage faith, the kind that springs right out of the pages of the Bible,
He's taken the ride that put the wind in his face and gave him the freedom
From this body of flesh to rise to all the promises of God in full flight.

His eyes see more majesty than he's witnessed in a lifetime here below
And his ears hear music much better than bands here in the sounds above.
The life he loved here and the zeal in which he lived now recedes
Because the life he knows now cannot compare with what he once knew.

The hero of our affections saw the sunshine in the darkest vale,
Who did not give way to complaint or self-pity, knows life beyond the sun.
He is missed. He is loved. His legacy lives on and makes us all rich in grace.
For those who knew and loved him he taught us how to do life right.

How do you say goodbye when you do not want to part with such a light?
You would give up the world to keep him and to walk all the way to the end.
The world needs such success stories, Who know the power of faith and love.
Why is it that the best of our age goes on and we struggle with what's left?

If we share Joseph's vintage faith in none other than Jesus we don't have to.
The Savior never leaves us. His presence is always very close and near.
Our sweetheart, son, and brother may be far away, but the way is clear,
And time is short to live our lives with the excellent spirit that Joseph did.

Joseph, thank you for loving the Savior so we never have to say goodbye.

This is the funeral message for this particular family. It serves as a sample for such a service. Most memorial services have two parts: one in the church and the other at the graveside.

Believe in God
(John 14:1–3)

I met Joseph last spring after a number of months of corresponding. We stood in the church parking lot. He was a picture of health, though he was already fighting the battle for his life then. His Uncle Daniel introduced us. Right away, I saw the excellent spirit and the vibrant faith that he had.

As a pastor, I look death in the face a lot. We might believe that death beat Joseph, but it did not. Joseph beat death with a victorious and relentless spirit. He walked through the dark vale and came out on the other side to the Father's house! He walked that vale with God who loved him.

He and his wife, Sarah, went to the place where many Americans once went to by reflex—to the Word of God. He wrote poems that were the fruit of deep reflection and struggles of the soul. He suffered. Yet these months have allowed him time to prepare for the door we will all walk through one day.

Look at what the Bible says to us here:

1. Let not your heart be troubled (John 14:1). He said it in such a way as if there was just one of us in heart-to-heart conversation with him. He knew trouble would come, but he did not want it to take us apart.

2. Jesus said, "Believe in God, believe also in me." Jesus was God in the flesh. We know that from John 14:9. Jesus beat death. Because he did, we can too (just as Joseph did).

3. We read that in the Father's house, there are many mansions. I do not want to disappoint you all, but the word mansions could be better translated as "rooms." But that shouldn't matter. It's the Father's House! He has prepared a place for you!

4. If he prepares that place, he has promised that he will come for you. He will come again so that where he is, there you may be also.

Notes

213

How about John 3:16?

Joey and Ruth understand that verse a lot better now. He gave his only begotten so that we might not perish, but have everlasting life. Right now that verse means the world to you. Believe God.

Then there is Romans 8:28, which says, "And we know that all things work together for good to them that love God, to them who are the called according to his purpose." Can you find the good in the death of a loved one? We might not see it yet, but all his works are good for those who love him and are called to his purpose. We don't feel good, but he will make it good. Believe God!

Philippians 4:6–8 had significance for Joseph and Sarah. These verses speak to those who believe God—not in a passive faith, but alive and active belief:

1. Don't be anxious about anything (Philippians 4:6). That covers a big world and a lot of hurt that you know all too well.

2. In every thing by prayer and supplication with thanksgiving let your requests be made known unto God (Philippians 4:6). That is setting things right and taking it to God so that you get through the heartache with him.

3. When we live and pray with a thankful heart, there is certain peace that passes all understanding. God will guard our hearts and minds.

4. Keep your mind on things that are honest, just, pure, lovely, and of good report, virtue, and praise. Do you see how that worked for the Harts? All they knew was heartache, bad reports, pain, yet out came praise!

Our belief in God is always tested in this world. If faith is passive, it is not vintage faith. If it is active, it is living and is the most powerful force in the world because it opens up the world to come.

Joseph showed us the world to come. He saw it before he went there. He had all the assurances and all the joys before he tasted them in full. He has become a hero of mine and yours because he loved the Lord despite his pain.

This was an additional poem written before the funeral service and his death that was read during the service:

Touching Blue Heaven
The Life and Testimony of Joseph Hart

I have a friend who looks into heaven.
His humility spills out, and his conversation runs deep.
In such valiant youth, death has fought hard against him.
Yet I witness his undefeatable spirit and firm resolve.

My brother has touched heaven and brought it down here.
His faith has, without doubt, come through as pure gold.
The fiery pain has hurt like hell, but all he sees is heaven.
Heaven has come near and been made real.

What is it in a man that oozes such sweetness?
It comes from above, where faith speaks to immortality.
The things of this earth recede when we see the heavenly.
We think life is about to end when really it just begins.

Life here below can be chock-full of sin and sorrow.
But the life above is unmatched in joy and wonder!
We want to stay with what we know here on this sod
While God calls us up to see those glories he prepared.

How can we touch blue heaven here on this green earth?
It is through a cherished brother, who is closer to home.
He sees what we cannot see and feels what we cannot feel.
His soul will be raptured, his golden faith live on!

Chapter 18

Deacon Ordination Service

What the Bible says about Deacon Ministry

Though it is not specified, the church draws from Acts 6:1–8:3 for their understanding about the early church and the appointment of deacons. The seven men named in Acts 6:5 were selected to give relief to widows and the apostles so they might give themselves to the Word and prayer (Acts 6:4).

1. There was murmuring in the early church because the Greek widows' needs were being neglected.
2. The apostles were resolute to committing their time to leading the people in the Word of God and prayer.
3. So they looked for men who were qualified as servant leaders to be sure that the needs of the people were met. They were men who were honest and full of the Holy Ghost and wisdom.
4. These men were set before the apostles. The church prayed and laid their hands upon these seven men with the charge to wait on tables.
5. Stephen's ministry is detailed:

    a. He was full of faith and power and did great miracles.

    b. The opposition was not able to resist his wisdom and spirit.

    c. When the opposition looked at him, they saw the face of an angel.

    d. He preached a sermon and made a strong personal appeal.

    e. He was full of the Holy Ghost. He saw the Lord at the right hand of God.

f. He became the church's first martyr as they stoned him in their rage.

g. He died with forgiveness and prayer on his lips for his accusers.

h. The bloodthirsty mob laid their cloaks at Saul of Tarsus's feet.

The one other passage the church looks to is 1 Timothy 3:8–13, where the qualifications of a deacon are detailed. A comparison can be made with the office of the bishop (overseer) in the first seven verses of the same chapter. The distinction is that one is set apart to lead and the other, to serve the church.

Practically speaking, deacons take care of the temporal, physical, and financial needs of the church. They are soul winners, church workers and prayer warriors. Their work is for the harmony of the church and the relief of the pastors. Deacons are Spirit-filled men who bless the men of God and the church family.

These are questions for a deacon candidate:

1. What do you depend on to save your soul from the penalty of your sins?

2. Do you know the essential truths of the Old and New Testament scriptures?

3. Would you say that you have a Christian worldview and lifestyle?

4. Is your marriage built on the principles found in Ephesians 5:21–33?

5. Have you been married one time? How about your wife? Are you both faithful to each other?

6. Do you lead your family in Christian devotions and Christian service?

Notes

217

7. Are your children well behaved and obedient to your instruction?

8. Would you say that you serve God more than money? Do you faithfully tithe?

9. Are you ever guilty of being double tongued? Is your wife free from slander?

10. Do you see the deacon as a servant and not as a ruler in the church?

11. Are you willing to serve and never to usurp the leadership of the pastor?

12. Have you been committed to witnessing and practical missions?

Deacon Ordination Service for Abel Shepherd

Opening Hymn and Choruses (Asaph Comfort, Worship Leader)

Prayer and Welcome (Pastor James Lamplighter)

Introduction of Shepherd Family and Deacons Special Music (Choral Group)

Personal Testimony of Faith by Abel Shepherd

Recommendation for Ordination (John Enoch, Deacon Leader)

Scripture Reading (1 Timothy 3:8-13)

Charge to the Church and Candidate (Pastor James Lamplighter)

Encouragement from the Deacon Ministry (Caleb Jordan, Deacon Leader)

Laying on of the Hands (Pastors and Deacons)

Presentation of Gifts (Shepherd Family)

Presentation of Ordination Bible (Pastor presents it to the candidate)

Hearty Hymn and Chorus of the Faith (Asaph Comfort, Worship Leader)

Chapter 19

Pastor Ordination Service

What the Bible says about Pastoral Ministry

The Bible calls the pastor, shepherd, elder, bishop, and overseer, a man of God. It is a designation of spiritual leadership like the prophets and apostles in biblical times. When men and women resisted them, murmured against them, and opposed them, they came under God's judgment.

Make no mistake, men of God today should be honored as such—as men sent from God. They should be carefully selected and be ready to serve in all wisdom and godliness. They should be filled with the Spirit, know the Word of God, and be soul-winners before their ordination.

First Timothy 3:1-7 and Titus 1:5-9 give these qualifications for a true man of God:

1. He desires good work (1 Timothy 3:1). We know from 1 Peter 5:4 that if he serves well, he will get a crown of glory that will never fade away!

2. The man of God must be blameless, the husband of one wife, vigilant, sober, well behaved, hospitable, and able to teach the Word of God (1 Timothy 3:2).

Notes

3. He is not to be a wine drinker, not a striker or violent, not greedy, patient, not a brawler or quarrelsome, and not covetous (1 Timothy 3:3).

4. The overseer is to rule his household well, having his children in subjection with all gravity or dignity (1 Timothy 3:4).

5. He is not to be a novice so that he is not given to pride and fall into the condemnation of the devil (1 Timothy 3:6).

6. The spiritual shepherd must have a good report in the community so that he does not fall into reproach or disgrace and the snare of the devil (1 Timothy 3:7).

7. He is to be a steward of God, not self-willed and given to anger. The man of God is to love good and righteous men, and be just, holy and temperate (Titus 1:7-8).

8. The pastor is to hold fast the faithful Word that he has been taught, so that he may be sound in doctrine and convince gainsayers (Titus 1:9).

These are questions for a pastor candidate:

1. When were you saved by grace, and how do you know you are regenerated?

2. Does your wife have saving grace, and does she share your calling?

3. Is your family an example of the faith? Are your children well behaved?

4. Are you both personally committed to the inerrancy of the Bible?

5. Does your family do practical ministry, missions, and Gospel outreach?

6. How do you deal with conflict, politics, and ungodliness in the church?

7. Are you a creationist? Do you believe in the literal view of Genesis?

8. Do you see it is essential to preach the Old Testament to understand grace?

9. How do you see the miracles of the Bible in the accounts of Exodus and Jonah?

10. Was the virgin birth necessary for salvation and justification of man?

11. Did Jesus bodily resurrect from the grave and forever defeat death?

12. Explain justification by faith and the meaning of the "free grace of God?"

13. Are hell and heaven literal places that all men will go to one day?

14. How do you see the sins of abortion, homosexuality, and fornication?

15. Would you be willing to marry a man and woman under all circumstances?

16. Do you believe in applying church discipline to errant members?

17. Are you willing to give up your ordination if you become disqualified?

18. Do you have courage to stand on the truth regardless of what it costs you?

19. How is your prayer life and intercession? Do you worship the Lord?

20. Does your heart burn to win souls and see believers encouraged?

Notes

Pastor Ordination Service for Josiah Cross

Opening Hymn and Choruses (Matthew Church, Worship Leader)

Prayer and Welcome (Pastor Joshua Free)

Introduction of the Cross Family and Pastors Special Music (Shepherds' Chorus)

Testimony of Salvation (Josiah Cross)

Brief Testimony (Melody Cross)

Recommendation for Ordination (Paul Evangel, Leader of Ordination Council)

Scripture Reading (Joshua 1:5-9, 1 Timothy 3:1-7, Titus 1:5-9)

Charge to the Church and Candidate (Pastor Jonathan Lamb)

Preaching the Word of the Lord (Candidate Josiah Cross)

Gospel Invitation (Candidate)

Laying on of the Hands (Pastors and Deacons)

Presentation of Gifts (Cross Family)

Presentation of Ordination Bible (Pastors make the presentation to the Candidate)

Hearty Hymn and Chorus of the Faith (Matthew Church, Worship Leader)

Closing prayer (Pastor Andrew Goodlight)

Chapter 20

Pastor Installation Service

Opening Hymn and Choruses (David Emmanuel, Worship Leader)

Prayer and Welcome (Pastor Peter Jamison)

Introduction of Pastor and Family
Pastors and Deacons Special Music (Miriam Brooks)

Testimony of Calling the Candidate (John Sweetwater)

Testimony of the Call of God to the Church (Micah Brooks)

Scripture Reading (Isaiah 61:1-3, 2 Timothy 4:1-8)

Profile of the Shepherd and His Sheep (Pastor Elias Temple)

Preaching the Word of the Lord (Pastor Micah Brooks)

Favorite Song of the Faith (David Emmanuel, Worship Leader)

Gospel Invitation (Pastor Micah Brooks)

Notes

Prayer of Blessing and Loyal Support (Pastors and Deacons)

Presentation of Gifts (Brooks Family)

Hearty Chorus (David Emmanuel, Worship Leader)

Closing Prayer (Pastor Nathan Grace)

Chapter 21

Transitional Pastoral Ministry

Pastors and churches have a variety of approaches for passing the baton of leadership on to the next overseer of the church. Some men of God will appoint their own successor. In other settings, the church wants a say, so they select a team of people to find an interim leader and then another to search for a long-term point man. This can be a challenging season for the people of God.

It is difficult because without a lead shepherd, all kinds of things can happen to upset the church. Ministry can suffer because leaders that are left with the responsibility to oversee the church do not always have the gifts to do so. People may cloak their motives and agendas in spiritual terms, but egos that want control often get into a tug-a-war with each other. Wise leadership is needed to prevent this.

Here are some principles to consider and steps to take in the time of transition:

1. No one is qualified and gifted to lead a church but a pastor, so be careful who is called and recognized as God-called pastors.

2. Deacons are not qualified and gifted to lead churches. They are servants only and not rulers of the house of God. The same goes for Bible teachers.

Notes

3. When it comes time to fill leadership positions during an interim time (the time in between lead pastors), interim leadership ought to be appointed by pastors.

4. The interim pastor must not have an agenda to get the church for his own. He should only serve for a short season and not undercut the search team.

5. Caution must be taken so that no associate pastor can seek the office by undercutting a prospective candidate before, during, or after the selection.

6. The search team should give prominent roles in making the selection to humble men of God who know the Bible, pray, and serve the church well.

7. In the absence of other pastors, the selection team should have members that have been loyal to the pastor and understand the gravity of the calling.

8. It is best not to elect the search team by popular vote because that in no way qualifies them to make such a crucial selection as the next pastor.

9. The elected church leaders who have high spiritual qualifications should select a search team with impartiality and much wisdom.

10. Candidates should be treated with courtesy, expenses should be paid to come to the church field, follow- ups should be done in a timely manner and terms of employment should be clear.

11. The search team should be forthright about the way the church works, the spiritual climate, and the levels of giving and support. Expectations should be explained.

12. It is best not to base the call on one day of sermons. The search team makes the recommendation, and the leaders and people affirm it.

13. The interim pastor and the incoming pastor can stabilize the church a great deal by spending time working together in visitation and outreach.

14. Men of God should not allow the previous pastor or the interim pastor undue influence so that the new pastor has the total support of the church.

15. The greatest asset a church can have in the transition period is courage to stand against egos and errors, and continue to do evangelism and equipping.

Notes

Chapter 22

Baptism

"Then cometh Jesus from Galilee to Jordan unto John, to be baptized of him. But John forbad him, saying, I have need to be baptized of thee, and comest thou to me? And Jesus answering said unto him, Suffer it to be so now: for thus it becometh us to fulfil all righteousness. Then he suffered him. And Jesus, when he was baptized, went up straightway out of the water: and, lo, the heavens were opened unto him, and he saw the Spirit of God descending like a dove, and lighting upon him: And lo a voice from heaven, saying, This is my beloved Son, in whom I am well pleased"
(Matthew 3:13-17).

Note the truths from this foundational text about baptism;

1. The Savior was baptized as an example to all who would follow and obey him. He did not need to be baptized for himself. He was baptized for us.

2. When we get baptized, we are fulfilling all righteousness.

3. When Jesus was baptized, he came up out of the water, which confirms the biblical mode of baptism.

4. As a result of this act in the life of the Master, the Spirit of God descended and the Father was pleased.

5. The three persons of God, who is one, were present at this event that began the ministry of Jesus.

A brief explanation of the trinity is helpful here: God is omnipresent, meaning that he is in all places at all times (including hell). He is one God manifested as three persons: God the Father in heaven, God the Son on earth and God the Holy Spirit indwelling the hearts of men. That is the nature of God. The Bible teaches the baptism of believers who have repented of their sins and placed their faith in the Lord Jesus. It is a symbolic act of obedience, not an act that saves. We do not affirm baptismal regeneration, but the regeneration of the Holy Spirit before baptism.

We do not get baptized for any other reason than to tell the world that the Lord has saved us. It is our public testimony of God's personal work in us.

We identify with Christ by full immersion, like a sunken ship, all of us goes under and what comes up is all of his!

It is a picture of the death, burial and resurrection of Jesus. As he died, we die to our sins, and as he arose, we arise to live a life for him and his service. When we bury our bodies in the watery grave, we bury carnality, worldliness and sinful desires for a life of obedience, faithfulness and full surrender.

There are many verses in the New Testament that affirms this teaching:

Therefore we are buried with him by baptism into death: that like as Christ
was raised up from the dead by the glory of the Father, even so we also
should walk in newness of life(Romans 6:4).

Buried with him in baptism, wherein also ye are risen with him through
the faith of the operation of God, who hath raised him from the dead
(Colossians 2:12).

The like figure whereunto even baptism doth also now save us (not the putting away of the filth of the flesh, but the answer of a good conscience toward God,) by the resurrection of Jesus Christ...(1 Peter 3:21).

The last verse is not an affirmation of baptism as a saving work when the context is understood. The reference is to Noah's ark in the previous verse. Noah's family was not saved by the water, but from the water. In the same way, believers are not saved by the water, but saved from the grave.

Baptism is the first public act of obedience. It does not wash away the filth of the flesh (how we wish), but it gives us the answer of a good conscience toward God because we have done what he said to do. Baptism is the beginning of our testimony of living for Christ, for his praise and glory, and by his life.

Notes

229

Chapter 23

The Lord's Supper

"*And as they were eating, Jesus took bread, and blessed it, and brake it, and gave it to the disciples, and said, Take, eat; this is my body. And he took the cup, and gave thanks, and gave it to them, saying, Drink ye all of it; For this is my blood of the new testament, which is shed for many for the remission of sins. But I say unto you, I will not drink henceforth of this fruit of the vine, until that day when I drink it new with you in my Father's kingdom. And when they had sung a hymn, they went out into the mount of Olives"* (Matthew 26:26-30).

There are three other passages that you can draw from to observe and teach the Lord's Supper: Mark 14:22-26; Luke 22:14-20; 1 Corinthians 11:20-34.

Note in Matthew's Gospel these simple truths:

1. Jesus and the disciples were together for the Passover. He became the Lamb that was slain just as John the Baptist foretold, "Behold the Lamb of God, which taketh away the sin of the world (John 1:29b).

2. Jesus was not teaching that they were actually eating his flesh and drinking his blood, but that they were symbols of his sacrifice.

3. It is noteworthy that John 6:48-58 is not a command to eat his flesh and drink his blood either, but to make his Word and teaching our bread and drink, to make his life our life as we walk in his steps. This is not cannibalism, but utter devotion to Jesus.

4. It is the New Testament covenant in the blood of Christ that gives the remission of sins.

5. The Lord said that he would not drink it again until he would drink it new with them in his Father's kingdom. That is the Marriage Supper of the Lamb (Revelation 19:9). Now he intercedes for the church. Then we will celebrate because he has taken us who were far away and drawn us near to have a place at the table of heaven when we deserve the torments of hell.

The Lord's Supper is not a sacrament (something that imparts divine grace). Grace by definition in the New Testament is an unmerited and unearned gift from God. The Supper is to commemorate the death of our Lord and the price he paid for our sins. The miracle is not what happens to the elements, but that we can be part of the Supper at all.

When we gather around the table in the local church, it is a time of spiritual examination according the 1 Corinthians 11:20-34. It is not a time to eat and drink as in a meal. It is a sacred time of thanksgiving and conviction. It is an opportunity to set things right in the fellowship in light of the blood of the cross. There is no better time to get the heart clean before the Lord.

It is best to build the service around the Lord's Supper and not to tack it on to the end of a service. Commemorate it often, not infrequently. Evangelical churches will observe it once a quarter, not often enough, especially since many members may miss the service when it is offered. It is not a time of frivolity, but a solemn time to reflect upon Calvary.

Notes

231

There is the question of open and closed communion that speaks to whether the table is for church members only or open to guests in the service. Each pastor must determine his own conviction under the leadership of the Holy Spirit. The pastor is the spiritual leader and under- shepherd of the local church. He governs these sacred moments.

We encourage believers to be obedient to baptism first before they take of the Lord's Supper. It is not a place for unbelievers, disbelievers, and those who are not living a life of repentance and faith. On our part, we do not practice closed communion where only church members can participate at the table. We practice open communion as long as the people see it as we do.

Here are the criteria: We come with clean hearts in view of the bread and fruit of the vine representing the broken body and shed blood of our Lord. We see no grace in receiving it, but as an act of obedience and faith to honor the Lord's death on our account. It is an ordinance for the local church where there is unleavened bread and the fruit of the vine taken in reverence and worship.

Chapter 24

Sample Sermon 1

Behold, the Lamb of God!
Isaiah 52:14; 53:1-13; John 1:29

The text in Isaiah 52 tells us that Jesus was beaten beyond recognition. It was if all the anger of man against God was taken out on him. The words in John 1:29 are those of John the Baptist when he saw Jesus. (He repeats them in John 1:36.)

1. **He was despised and rejected of men (Isaiah 53:3).**

   a. We live in a different world than Jesus and the apostles did. Whatever they did in preaching and ministry caused rejection. He was called the man of sorrows. They hid their faces from him. They were ashamed to be associated with him! All our sins and all hell's fury came against him.

   b. They esteemed him not. This is the one man who should have had hero worship and the highest praise, but he was locked out of their hearts. Here is how John 1:11 says it:"He came unto his own, and his own received him not." When he suffered, he suffered for our sins.

Notes

2. **He was smitten of God and afflicted (Isaiah 53:4).**

    a. He bore our griefs and carried our sorrows. There is no hurt that you can have that does not pain him. There are no tears you can shed that he has not first shed. He loved us so much that he became one of us. The heart of God has known pain, but still he went on and put on robes of flesh to feel the very sting of sin.

    b. He was not esteemed—but was stricken, smitten, and afflicted. Stricken means "to strike violently." The word smitten implies beating and wounding. Where is the wounding, beating and violence coming from? God. He laid our stripes upon him. He took the beating meant for us. He bled for us!

3. **He was wounded for our transgressions (Isaiah 53:5, 8, 12).**

    a. The word transgression is found in verses 5, 8, and 12. It is "revolt and rebellion against God or another." When we rebel against the Word of God, it is a high offense against heaven. The result is Golgotha. We take sin very lightly. We wink at it. But it wounded Jesus. It crucified him. It pierced him!

    b. Take a look at verse 12. He was numbered with the transgressors, yet he made intercession for them. He bore the sin of many. Those sins broke his body and turned his heart into water and blood. I have been to places where I was treated as royalty when I'm not. He was and is so much more. Yet he still came for us!

4. **He gave his life as an offering for sin (Isaiah 53:10).**

    a. Note the following lines with me: We read twice in verse 7 that "He openeth not his mouth" (1 Peter 2:22–23). Verse 9 says, "He had done no violence, neither was any deceit in his mouth." Then we see verse 10, which says, "Yet it pleased the Lord to bruise him." Because he loved you more than him!

    b. He did what Moses and Paul wanted to do— gave his very life for his people. He loved to the uttermost! So in light of that, never doubt his care for you! Do you know Romans 8:32 and Isaiah 53:11? It says that he shall see the travail of his soul because he will justify (it means "declared right!") many. He will bear their iniquities.

Verse 12 states, "He hath poured out his soul unto death." In clear terms, God became flesh and took your beating, wounds, griefs, and sorrows so you would not have to. He took your death so you would not have to die. Jesus came for you!

This picture of Jesus is clear to us as Christians, but Jews today see it as a picture of the sufferings of Israel. It is an incredible misinterpretation, but they must dismiss Jesus. What they do in the process is fulfill this very text.

We too can dismiss Jesus if we do not see why he died and what he came to do. He died for sin, and he came to show his glory in you. You are not a dead end for his blessings. You are a channel and conduit to the cross.

Gospel Invitation: Repent. Place your faith in Jesus alone and surrender your will to do the will of God regardless of the cost (Matthew 16:24).

Notes

Sample Sermon 2

How to be Sure about Your Salvation
(1 John 5:11–13)

A parachute company that faithfully packed most of the manufactured parachutes in the market found a way to pack faster, but their rate for proper deployment dropped drastically. Their sales greatly increased, but so did the fatalities. Would you buy from the company if they had a 10 percent success rate?

That is just about the deployment rate of Christians! Of all the people that say they know the Lord, that have made the steps of faith and been baptized, about 10 percent succeed in living out the Christian life and do not go back to the world. Something is wrong with the parachute. Something is wrong with the message.

Many will say that you cannot know for sure. No one knows until they get there. The Bible says otherwise right here. This is how you can know for sure:

1. **Your sins are forgiven (1 John 1:7–9).**

    a. Walk in the light. When we walk in the light, we do not hide our sins in the dark. Light shows us for what we are, what we do, and how we act.

    b. Have fellowship with one another. When our hearts are right, we get along! We keep no record of wrong. Fellowship is more than just getting along. It is partnership for the Gospel, a rare trait in today's "selfy culture."

    c. Confess your sins. Here is how it is spelled out in James 5:14–16. The context is prayer for

236

the sick, but the "how to" speaks about confession. You have had a full reality check with the law of God and know your guilt and conviction. Now, that nagging guilt is gone. You no longer have anything to hide, nothing that you are ashamed for others to know about. Your heart is clean. You are forgiven, and it is the greatest feeling on earth.

2. **You keep his commands (1 John 2:3–6).**

   a. Keep his Word. We know that we know him if we obey him. Have you ever seen Acts 5:32? Why is the Holy Spirit a stranger in our midst, or why are we not constantly being filled with his joy and presence? Obedience is the answer!

   b. Walk as he walked. If you don't obey, the truth is not in you. We can go further than that: if you don't obey, his love is not in you! We know we are in him when we walk as he did. We remind people of Jesus.

   c. Do righteousness (1 John 2:28–29; 3:7, 10). Those who abide in the Lord do what is right. When we are born again, born from above, born of him, we do right! Obeying the Lord is no longer like pulling teeth. It is your joy to do what he says. You do not excuse yourself because of gifting, age, time, or comfort. You know what the Bible says you must do. When you hear the truth, you're ready to line up your life by it. You do it because you love him.

3. **You have the Holy Ghost (1 John 3:24; 4:13).**

   a. Romans 8:9 says, "Now if any man have not the Spirit of Christ, he is none of his." There is life inside! There is conviction. When you sin, you know it, and you cannot live with it and be at peace. He makes you his temple.

Notes

b. First Corinthians 6:19–20 says it well. When we have saving grace, the Holy Spirit of God has us. We do not possess him. He possesses us!

c. John 6:37 is a verse to remember: "him that cometh to me I will in no wise cast out." We do not come to him clean or right or perfect. We come needy, dirty, and sinful. He receives us, forgives us, and keeps us by his grace! The Spirit of God lives in you! When you do wrong, he speaks and convicts. When you need insight and understanding, he teaches. When you seek to know the will of God, he directs and guides. You know you are his because there is the unmistakable presence of the Lord always at work in you.

4. **You love God and the brothers (1 John 4:7–8, 16, 21; 5:2–3).**

a. We love. If you have a problem with hate, you have a problem with God! Agape love is God's kind of love. It is unconditional. Only God can give it and the people of God. They have done so against great odds and affliction.

b. We love each other. The test of love is not so much in loving God, who can be defined in your own terms, but it's learning to love the unlovable, annoying, and undesirable. That is what we were before he loved us!

c. We love God enough to keep his commands. If we cannot love our brothers, then we are strangers to the love of God. He commands that you love.

Here may be the biggest test of all: when you say you love God, you know you do because you love the brethren. You know it is sheer hypocrisy to proclaim your love and devotion to God but hate, mistreat, or be unwilling to forgive your brother. You know—you know him because he gives you grace to love.

You're going to take a jump someday out of this life into the next. That is when the resurrection life will make all the difference in the world. Nothing will help you then but a living faith that's tried by the fires of this life in suffering, affliction, and tribulation. When that time comes, it will not be all about you but him.

Jesus preached about "the key of knowledge" in Luke 11:52. Jesus was God in the flesh. The lawyers in the Lord's Day knew the law of God, the character of God, and honored the name of God, but did not know God! When Jesus came, they did not know him. What is the key to knowledge? It is truth. Jesus is Truth!

You can be sure of saving grace when you know you are forgiven, obedient, full of the Spirit of God and not the world, and when you keep saying "yes" to love!

When I was a young Christian, one of my heroes was Corrie Ten Boom. She came face to face at one of her speaking engagements with the Nazi guard who had tormented her and her sister Betsie in the detention camp. The hate of those years filled her heart. So what was she to do? He was remorseful and needed forgiveness. She was struggling. Right there, God melted her heart!

Sample Sermon 3

Humility
James 4:6, 10; 1 Peter 5:5-6

It is the hardest of all the Christian virtues to apply and the key to the rest of them. What is it that if you were to get it and rejoice to have it, you would lose it again? It's humility! Humility opens a double wide door to God's favor. It is a rare find among people today. Most everyone loves a humble soul.

Humility hides you from the view of men but places you in the direct vision of God. We have four verses here that tell us about humility from God's perspective. There is no greater example than the Lord Jesus, who was all of God and all of man—except the sin of man. He humbled himself because of his love for man. He stepped way down!

1. **God gives more grace to the humble (James 4:6).**

    a. He gives all *common* grace. Each us have air to breathe whether we worship and honor God or not. It is his breath in us! He guards our steps. He provides our necessities. He is the giver of every good and perfect gift (James 1:17).

b. He offers *uncommon* grace to those who hear the Gospel and believe in Jesus. A whole new world opens up for those who know the power of grace (Ephesians 2:8-10).

c. He gives greater *uncommon* grace to those who walk before him in humility (Isaiah 6:5; 64:6). If you will be humble, you will see windows and doors to heaven open! This truth is quoted from the Old Testament (Proverbs 3:34; 29:23; Mal. 3:10).

2. Humble yourself in the sight of God (James 4:10).

a. There are some men who see God before they (physically) see God. Isaiah did. All of the prophets did. Righteous kings did. The true apostles did. Ladies of grace did. Let me give you an example through the prophet Micah (Mic. 6:8).

b. Psalm 75:7 says, "But God is the judge: he putteth down one, and setteth up another." Let him lift you up! This is a promise: when we humble ourselves, he shall lift us up! Remember the admonition in Luke 14:8-11.

c. The Bible says in Numbers 12:3, "Now the man Moses was very meek above all the men which were upon the face of the earth." What is the distinction between meekness and humility? Meekness implies forbearance, strength under control. Humility is to be lowly and modest.

3. Be clothed with humility (1 Peter 5:5).

a. "Submit yourselves unto the elder." That is a term for a pastor or leader of the church, but that is not the meaning here. In the context of the passage, it refers to an older man. (The Lord smote my heart over this when I was a young pastor.)

b. "Be subject one to another..." You will find a string of three pearls in Romans 12:3, 10, 16 that all speak to the way we are to relate to each other in the church. This is the "fashion" in the church. It's humility!

c. "God resisteth the proud, and giveth grace to the humble." All of us would affirm that the chief trait in the church is agape love, but the way that trait works is through humility. If we love each other, we will "be clothed in humility."

4. Humble yourselves under the mighty hand of God (1 Peter 5:6).

a. We humble ourselves that he may exalt us in due time. This reference is very much like James 4:10. Pride will take us down, but humility lifts us up (Prov. 16:18; 18:12). We call you up to humility!

b. The words due time refer to the proper set time appointed by the Lord. Years ago, a Baptist preacher who had been a high school football player from West Palm Beach, Florida, went out on the football field to pray. He dug a hole, lay on the earth, and put his nose in the hole. This is what he said, "Lord, this is as low as I can go. Please bless me. "That young man was Adrian Rogers—a beloved pastor from Memphis, Tennessee.

c. We want to be unlike the devil (Isaiah 14:12-14)— free of ego and selfish ambition. We want to be like Jesus who is aptly described in Matthew 11:28-30.

Johnson Oatman Jr. penned these words and George Hugg, the music:

"No, Not One"

There's not a friend like the lowly Jesus
No, not one! No, not one!
None else could heal all our soul's diseases
No, not one! No, not one!

Chorus:

Jesus knows all about our struggles He will guide till the day is done There's not a friend like the lowly Jesus No, not one! No, not one!

No friend like him is so high and holy
No, not one! No, not one!
And yet no friend is so meek and lowly
No, not one! No, not one!

(Chorus)

There's not an hour that he is not near us
No, not one! No, not one!
No night so dark, but his love can cheer us
No, not one! No, not one!

241

Notes

(Chorus)

Did ever saint find this friend forsake him?
No, not one! No, not one!
Or sinner find that he would not take him?
No, not one! No, not one!

(Chorus)

Was ever a gift like the Savior given?
No, not one! No, not one!
Will he refuse us a home in heaven?
No, not one! No, not one!

(Chorus)

How do we get past the lessons on humility and get in the circle of blessing? How do we get humble? We have to win the battle of the mind and be humble in heart. We can only be humble if we stay close to the cross. The more pride we have, the further we are from the cross. We must choose Jesus or the devil.

Here are four things that the humble will do when it comes to practical service:

1. They will find a way to serve and share their faith out of humble gratitude.

2. They will give their heart for the church, the Gospel, and the kingdom because the epitome of humility did just that—Jesus laid down his life to save and rescue man.

3. They will love people like the lost and discouraged more than themselves.

4. They will spend enough time on their knees to keep their pride in check.

This kind of humility was seen in Christmas Evans. He brought a wealthy agnostic to the Lord when no one else could. The man said he had never met anyone so humble and so sure of his faith. Christmas could not speak plain and could not look people straight in the eye, but he melted the heart of the agnostic because of his humility!

Part IX

Conclusion:
When We Stand
Before the Chief Shepherd

There may be no better words for a shepherd as he considers his future accountability than those in 1 Peter 5:1–11:

> *The elders which are among you I exhort, who am also an elder, and a witness of the sufferings of Christ, and also a partaker of the glory that shall be revealed: Feed the flock of God which is among you, taking the oversight thereof, not by constraint, but willingly; not for filthy lucre, but of a ready mind; Neither as being lords over God's heritage, but being examples to the flock. And when the chief Shepherd shall appear, ye shall receive a crown of glory that fadeth not away. Likewise, ye younger, submit yourselves unto the elder. Yea, all of you be subject one to another, and be clothed with humility: for God resisteth the proud, and giveth grace to the humble. Humble yourselves therefore under the mighty hand of God, that he may exalt you in due time: Casting all your care upon him; for he careth for you. Be sober, be vigilant; because your adversary the devil, as a roaring lion, walketh about, seeking whom he may devour: Whom resist stedfast in the faith, knowing that the same afflictions are accomplished in your brethren that are in the world. But the God of all grace, who hath called us unto his eternal glory by Christ Jesus, after that ye have suffered a while, make you perfect, stablish, strengthen, settle you. To him be glory and dominion for ever and ever. Amen.*

Shepherds who have served well in keeping with these lines have the promise of a crown of glory that never fades. What is even more remarkable is who gives the crown: the chief Shepherd.

Let this world fade for a moment and think of eternity when faith will be sight and all that Christians believe about the Bible and the Savior will be true. All the heartbreak, pain, agony of soul, rivers of tears that God collected in his bottle (Psalms 56:8), false accusation, mockery, and ridicule, every attack, rejection, and revolts against the Word of God—All of it will be put to rest before God.

Every whispered prayer, each late night visit in the hospital, and all the witnessing done will come to light on the Day of the Lord. Nothing will be forgotten:—no act, no sacrifice, no intercession, no sermon.

Note Galatians 6:7–9:

> *Be not deceived; God is not mocked: for whatsoever a man soweth, that shall he also reap. For he that soweth to his flesh shall of the flesh reap corruption; but he that soweth to the Spirit shall of the Spirit reap life everlasting. And let us not be weary in well doing: for in due season we shall reap, if we faint not.*

The harvest of every deed done for the glory of God will be fully rewarded.

Cast not away therefore your confidence, which hath great recompence of reward. (Hebrews 10:35)

Look to yourselves, that we lose not those things which we have wrought, but that we receive a full reward. (2 John 1:8)

It is sin to live for the comfort of today. The small sacrifices that are made have eternal impact on the needy whom the faithful serve. Men toil over their houses and forget about the house they should be building above. They fret over reputation and do not remember that the Lord "made himself of no reputation" (Philippians 2:7). See the contrast of this life and the next in 2 Corinthians 4:16–18:

For which cause we faint not; but though our outward man perish, yet the inward man is renewed day by day. For our light affliction, which is but for a moment, worketh for us a far more exceeding and eternal weight of glory; While we look not at the things which are seen, but at the things which are not seen: for the things which are seen are temporal; but the things which are not seen are eternal.

Time is limited, but the reward in eternity is forever. There is only a little while to serve the Lord in this flesh, to fight the fight, and to give him glory when all hell seems to go against the servants of the Lord because they bear the light, truth, and hope of the world. Everywhere there are people who call themselves by his name and say that they are his servants, when in reality, they have lost their way.

Notes

The Word of God is our inspiration, and the Spirit of God is our strength.

> *There remaineth therefore a rest to the people of God. For he that is entered into his rest, he also hath ceased from his own works, as God did from his. Let us labour therefore to enter into that rest, lest any man fall after the same example of unbelief. For the word of God is quick, and powerful, and sharper than any twoedged sword, piercing even to the dividing asunder of soul and spirit, and of the joints and marrow, and is a discerner of the thoughts and intents of the heart. Neither is there any creature that is not manifest in his sight: but all things are naked and opened unto the eyes of him with whom we have to do. (Hebrews 4:9-13)*

Men of God and ladies of grace have the high calling of bringing people into the presence of the Lord. If the people see the manifest presence of God, they will be compelled to lay aside any pretense and be found true in his sight.

If leaders will serve daily in his presence, then there will be no surprise for them or their people because his Word will fully prepare them for what is to come. The same Holy Spirit who is interceding for them and teaching all things, will make them ready for heaven. The truth of 1 John 4:17 comes to light:

> *Herein is our love made perfect, that we may have boldness in the day of judgment: because as he is, so are we in this world. There is no fear in love; but perfect love casteth out fear: because fear hath torment. He that feareth is not made perfect in love.*

Christians will have boldness at the judgment because they can be confident that in their lifetime, they loved him truly.

It seems preposterous to think that anyone could be ready for heaven, to stand before the presence of God— but for those who live close to the Word of God and walk by the Spirit of God, it can be true. There is no moral or spiritual perfection on this earth, but hearts can be tried by the truth and aligned with the Spirit of truth daily so that like Enoch, they can just step into heaven!

> *And Enoch walked with God: and he was not; for God took him. (Gen. 5:24)*

Do not live for this world, but live for the moment when all will stand before the Lord. He is, after all is said and done, life's reward.

Hebrews 11:6 is the standard of faith and expectancy:

> *But without faith it is impossible to please him: for he that cometh to God must believe that he is, and that he is a rewarder of them that diligently seek him.*

For the tribe of Levi, there were no allotments of land for them to inherit in the Promised Land, only villages for their families to inhabit. God was their portion.

At that time the Lord separated the tribe of Levi, to bear the ark of the covenant of the Lord, to stand before the Lord to minister unto him, and to bless in his name, unto this day. Wherefore Levi hath no part nor inheritance with his brethren; the Lord is his inheritance, according as the Lord thy God promised him. (Deuteronomy 10:8-9)

Never forget that in the hard terrain of this world, believers stand before the Lord to minister in his name. He is their portion. The standard is never the world's acclaim. The religious elite and the powers of this world will treat them like they did the Lord. If the world does not come against Christians today, then they must pay the price to recover the message of faith and repentance.

Men of God are those who keep the light of the Gospel shining bright in the church, and ladies of grace are those who light the torches by their prayers and examples of faith. Every generation of leaders is called to fight ungodliness and error so that the Gospel shines. (There is always a price to pay to keep the light bright.)

The true Gospel will always challenge the darkness, so fight to stay close to the Word! The distance between the church and the truth of the scripture is the distance between the people and the blessing of God. Such blessing is not an easy road: it may be filled with want and hurt, but there will be incalculable eternal fruit and glory to God. The Lord of the ages is not after leisure but likeness to the Son, for there is no one like him!

When shepherds and godly ladies stand before him, they want to know that they reflected his glory on the earth. Their heart is to give him such praise that it matches the honor he receives in heaven. They want to know that they did not idolize the things of this world, personal ego, and fleshly demands. For they know praise only counts if it comes from him.

Notes

Therefore judge nothing before the time, until the Lord come, who both will bring to light the hidden things of darkness, and will make manifest the counsels of the hearts: and then shall every man have praise of God. (1 Corinthians 4:5)

Bibliography

Alcorn, Randy. *The Purity Principle*. Colorado Springs: Multnomah Books, 2003.

———. *The Treasure Principle*. Colorado Springs: Multnomah Books, 2005.

Bridges, Jerry. *The Practice of Godliness*. Colorado Springs: Navpress Publishing Group, 1989.

———. *The Pursuit of Holiness*. Colorado Springs: Navpress Publishing Group, 1989.

Cahill, Mark. *One Heartbeat Away: Your Journey into Eternity*. Biblical Discipleship Publishers, 2005.

———. *One Thing You Can't Do in Heaven*. Rockwall: Biblical Discipleship Publishers, 2002.

Coleman, Robert. *Master Plan of Evangelism*. Grand Rapids: Fleming H. Revell Company, 1993.

Dallimore, Arnold. George Whitefield. Wheaton: CrosswayBooks, 2010.

Dever, Mark. *Nine Marks of a Healthy Church*. Wheaton: Crossway Books, 2004.

Edwards, Jonathan. *The Diary and Journal of David Brainerd*. Carlisle: The Banner of Truth Trust, 2007.

———. *Resolutions and Advice to Young Converts*. Cedar Lake: Readaclassic.com, 2011.

Grubb, Norman. *C.T. Studd*. Fort Washington: Christian Literature Crusade, 1982.

———. Rees Howells, *Intercessor*. Fort Washington: Christian Literature Crusade, 1988.

Johnstone, Patrick. *Operation World*. Toronto: Gabriel Resources, 2001.

MacArthur, John. *The Gospel According to Jesus*. Grand Rapids: Zondervan Publishing Company, 2008.

———. *The MacArthur New Testament Commentary*. Chicago: Moody Publishers, 1991–2015.

———. *Strange Fire*. Katy: Nelson Books, 2013.

Phillips, John. *The John Phillips Commentary Series*. Grand Rapids: Kregel Publications, 1974–2004.

Pierson, Arthur. *George Muller of Bristol*. Peabody: Hendrickson Publishers, 2008.

Piper, John. *Don't Waste Your Life*. Wheaton: Crossway Books, 2007.

———. *Let the Nations Be Glad*. Ada: Baker Academic, 2003.

Ravenhill, Leonard. *Revival Praying*. Bloomington: Bethany House Publishers, 2005.

———. *Why Revival Tarries*. Bloomington: Bethany House Publishers, 1979.

Taylor, Howard. *Hudson Taylor's Spiritual Secret*. Chicago: Moody Publishers, 1955

.

About the Authors

Lon Chenowith is the Director of Missions of Sandy Run Baptist Association in Bostic, North Carolina. He has served as a church planter and pastor for thirty years and evangelized and trained in twenty-three nations. He and his wife Kay reside in Forest City, North Carolina. They have two sons, a daughter, four grandsons, and two granddaughters. He loves to run, mountain bike, and hike the backcountry from the Appalachians to the Rockies.

Kay Chenowith takes joy in teaching the Bible to ladies. She has been a summer missionary to Native Americans, worked at every level in church life, led youth mission teams, organized county-wide National Days of Prayer, trained international pastors' wives, and she loves hospitality in the home. She believes in the power of intercessory prayer. Kay delights in her sons, daughter, daughters-in-law and grandchildren.

Made in the USA
Columbia, SC
26 January 2024

30289270R00146